Marijuana 360

Marijuana 360

Differing Perspectives on Legalization

Nancy E. Marion and
Joshua B. Hill

ROWMAN & LITTLEFIELD
Lanham • Boulder • New York • London

Published by Rowman & Littlefield
A wholly owned subsidiary of
The Rowman & Littlefield Publishing Group, Inc.
4501 Forbes Boulevard, Suite 200, Lanham, Maryland 20706
www.rowman.com

6 Tinworth Street, London SE11 5AL, United Kingdom

British Library Cataloguing in Publication Information Available

Library of Congress Cataloging-in-Publication Data

Names: Marion, Nancy E., author. | Hill, Joshua B., author.
Title: Marijuana 360 : differing perspectives on legalization / Nancy E. Marion and Joshua B. Hill.
Description: Lanham, Maryland : Rowman & Littlefield, 2019. | Includes bibliographical references and index.
Identifiers: LCCN 2018047692 (print) | LCCN 2018048082 (ebook) | ISBN 9781442281660 (electronic) | ISBN 9781442281653 (cloth : alk. paper)
Subjects: LCSH: Marijuana—Law and legislation—United States. | Drug Legalization—United States.
Classification: LCC KF3891.M2 (ebook) | LCC KF3891.M2 M35 2019 (print) | DDC
   345.73/0277—dc23
LC record available at https://lccn.loc.gov/2018047692

Printed in the United States of America

Contents

Chapter One

Public Support for Legalization

The public's attitudes toward marijuana use have changed dramatically in recent years throughout the United States. In the 1930s, many people believed that marijuana was more dangerous and more deadly than substances such as opium, morphine, and heroin. Since then, public support for marijuana legalization has turned around.[1] More people agree that marijuana is a safe substance for use, even safer than legal substances like alcohol or tobacco. Many agree that marijuana has medical qualities that can relieve symptoms of a wide variety of ailments. Many others agree that it can be used recreationally to help people relax after a tough day or even to stimulate creativity in some individuals.

The public's perceptions of marijuana have been tracked over time. Public opinion can be thought of as the "shared opinion of a collection of individuals on a common concern,"[2] or a compilation of how the general public feels about an issue.[3] The Gallup polling organization carried out an early poll on the public's perception of marijuana legalization in 1969. The question asked was, "Do you think the use of marijuana should be made legal or not?" The results indicated that only 12 percent of respondents were in favor of legalization. A similar poll taken a few years later showed that the percentage of respondents supporting marijuana had increased to 28 percent. The support for legal marijuana fell during the 1980s, possibly due to President Reagan's War on Drugs. The percentage of people who supported legal marijuana remained at about 25 percent through the mid-1990s but in 2000 increased significantly to 31 percent.[4] A more recent poll taken in 2013 indicated that the public support for legislation rose dramatically to 58 percent. Table 1.1 shows the results of

Table 1.1.   Support for Marijuana Legalization

Year	Percent Supporting Legalization
1969	12
1973	16
1977	28
1985	23
2001	34
2005	36
2009	44
2013	58

Source: Swift, A. (2016, October 19). "Support for Legal Marijuana Use up to 60 percent in U.S. Gallup Research." www.gallup.com/poll/196550/support-legal-marijuana.aspx.

public opinion polls about marijuana legalization over time. More information on how Gallup carries out their polls is presented in box 1.1.

Polls taken by other organizations show similar trends to those found by the Gallup organization. The Pew Research Organization took an early poll on marijuana legalization in 1969, asking respondents if they believed that marijuana should be either legal or remain illegal. Their results showed that only 12 percent supported legalization (see table 1.2). Since that early poll, support for marijuana legalization has risen dramatically, peaking at 57 percent in 2016.[5]

Public opinion polls carried out by the AP-NORC Center for Public Affairs Research in 2016 reported that about 61 percent of Americans

Table 1.2.   Pew Survey: Do You Think the Use of Marijuana Should Be Made Legal?

Date	Legal	Illegal
1969	12	84
1980	30	66
1990	16	81
2000	31	63
2006	32	60
2016	57	37

Source: Geiger, A. (2016, October 12). "Support for Marijuana Legalization Continues to Rise." Pew Research Center. www.pewresearch.org/fact-tank/2016/10/12/support-for-marijuana-legalization-continues-to-rise.

TEXTBOX 1.1. HOW POLLS ARE TAKEN

Public opinion polls are used to identify the public's ideas and perceptions of issues, people, and events. They can be used to track patterns locally, nationally, or even internationally. Polls can be completed in person, over the phone, or by a mailed or paper survey. However the information is gathered, a poll that is carried out using scientific methods can be an accurate reflection of the public's mood. Pollsters need not question every person in a population in order to get a reliable estimate of opinions. Instead, they can interview only a small group of the entire population, analyze those responses, and generalize to the entire population. If the sample is chosen correctly, it can be a reliable measure of the entire population. It is imperative that the people questioned comprise a "representative sample," meaning that all categories of people are represented in the smaller sample. The potential respondents must be randomly selected from the entire population in a process called probability sampling. For example, when it comes to telephone surveys, Gallup uses a random-digit-dialing (RDD) technique that provides them with a random list of phone numbers (cell phones and landlines). This means that the phone numbers are not chosen based on any characteristic: age, location, income, or any other attribute. The questions that are asked must also be written in such a way that the responses are not biased, allowing the respondents' answers to be a true reflection of their views. Some of the more well-recognized organizations known for conducting trustworthy polls include Gallup, Pew, Rasmussen, CNN, *New York Times*/CBS, Harris, and Quinnipiac University.

favored marijuana legalization. When questioned further, 24 percent of those in favor of legalization thought that marijuana should be available only with a physician's recommendation. Moreover, about 43 percent indicated that laws should place limits on the amount of marijuana that users can purchase.[6]

Most people who support marijuana legalization do so because of the possible medical benefits of the plant. The second most prevalent reason for support pertains to the safety of marijuana as a natural drug. On the other hand, those who oppose marijuana report that they are concerned about the addictive qualities of the drug.[7] Others report that marijuana causes harm to society in general and therefore should not be legal.[8]

As the support for legal marijuana increases, overall support for the War on Drugs has declined. Those who oppose the War on Drugs indicate that it has been, or continues to be, a waste of money.[9]

As table 1.3 shows, a respondent's age affects his or her level of support for marijuana legalization. Those respondents between the ages of eighteen and thirty-four, otherwise known as the millennial generation, have higher support for legalization. Those who are fifty-five years and older tend to have the lowest amount of support for legalization. In 2017, about 71 percent of young respondents indicated that they supported legalization of marijuana (see table 1.4). Those born in the early to mid-1960s had the second-highest level of support, at 57 percent. This population is referred to as the Gen X generation. The "baby boomers" have about the same level of support, around 56 percent.[10] As expected, older Americans in general have the least amount of support for legalization.

Table 1.4 also shows that support for marijuana legalization is found more in males than females and more in Democrats than Republicans. Independents show even more support. More information is provided in tables 1.6 and 1.7.

More recent polls have found that the number of people who believe that marijuana can be harmful to users has decreased during the past twenty-five years. Results from polls taken in 1991 showed that about 84

Table 1.3. Support for Marijuana by Age

	2003/2005	*2016*
National Adults	35%	60%
18–34	44%	77%
35–54	35%	61%
55+	29%	45%

Source: Swift, A. (2016, October 19). "Support for Legal Marijuana Use up to 60 percent in U.S. Gallup Research." www.gallup.com/poll/196550/support-legal-marijuana.aspx.

Table 1.4. Support for Marijuana

	Legal	Illegal	Unsure
Total	57%	37%	5%
Men	60%	34%	5%
Women	55%	40%	5%
White	59%	36%	5%
Black	59%	37%	4%
Hispanic	46%	49%	5%
Millennial (18–35)	71%	25%	5%
Gen X (35–51)	57%	38%	5%
Baby Boomer (52–70)	56%	40%	4%
Postgrad	60%	33%	7%
College Grad	59%	37%	4%
Some College	63%	32%	5%
High School or Less	53%	42%	5%
Republican	41%	55%	5%
Conservative Republican	33%	62%	5%
Moderate/Liberal Republican	63%	35%	3%
Independent	63%	33%	5%
Democrat	66%	30%	4%
Conservative/Moderate Democrat	55%	39%	5%
Liberal Democrat	78%	19%	3%

Source: Geiger, A. (2016, October 12). "Support for Marijuana Legalization Continues to Rise." Pew Research Center. www.pewresearch.org/fact-tank/2016/10/12/support-for-marijuana-legalization-continues-to-rise. Survey conducted August 23–September 2, 2016, Pew Research Center.

Table 1.5. Support for Legalizing the Use of Marijuana, by Birth Cohort, over Time

	1969	1985	2000/2001	2015
1981–1997	NA	NA	NA	71
1966–1980	NA	NA	43	64
1951–1965	NA	32	35	58
1936–1950	20	22	29	40
1935 and earlier	8	15	18	19

Source: Jones, Jeffrey M. (2015, October 21) "In U.S., 58% Back Legal Marijuana Use." *Social & Policy Issues*, Gallup http//newsgallup.com/poll/186260/back-legal-marijuana.asp.

Table 1.6. Support for Marijuana by Political Party Affiliation

	2003/2005	2016
National Adults	35	60
Republicans	20	42
Independents	46	70
Democrats	38	67

Source: Swift, A. (2016, October 19). "Support for Legal Marijuana Use up to 60 percent in U.S. Gallup Research." www.gallup.com/poll/196550/support-legal-marijuana.aspx.

Table 1.7. Support for Marijuana Legalization by Political Party

	Should	Should Not	Unsure/No Answer
Total	59	36	5
Republicans	35	61	4
Democrats	72	23	5
Independents	58	36	5
May 24–30, 2016	54	41	5
November 28–December 12, 2012	51	44	5

Source: Quinnipiac University Poll, February 16–21, 2017. www.pollingreport.com/drugs.htm. N=1,323 registered voters nationwide.

percent of the public perceived marijuana to be harmful to users. In 2014, that number dropped to about 53.8 percent.[11]

The public's support for marijuana was made evident in the state of Washington, where voters approved marijuana use in 2012. Four years after the original vote, a polling organization asked voters if they would cast the same or a different vote if given the chance to vote again on the initiative to legalize marijuana. The results found that more than 25 percent of voters who were originally opposed to the legalization of marijuana reported that they would change their position and now vote in favor. Moreover, the results showed that older voters with at least a bachelor's degree and who had a history of using marijuana were most likely to support legalization.[12] The public support for marijuana in Washington could not be clearer.

CURRENT BOOK

These polls show clearly that public opinion about marijuana has changed over time and that it differs by age, gender, race, education, and political party affiliation. These changes have led to new policies to legalize marijuana in some form. This book is an analysis of the public's opinions about marijuana with a focus on individual professions. Many professions will be impacted in different ways by the legalization of marijuana. Teachers, police officers, and medical professionals must face problems that result from the new policies. Each chapter that follows provides an analysis of how different professionals, as a group, feel about the legalization of medical and recreational marijuana. The data was collected through a series of interviews, both in person and written, in which the professionals were asked about their perceptions of how legislation legalizing marijuana would affect them and their jobs. The goal was to provide a deeper understanding of not only how marijuana will affect society as a whole, but how different professionals will have to adapt their daily tasks to accommodate the new environment.

In chapters 2 and 3, a short description of the history and current status of marijuana legalization are provided. Chapter 4 presents some of the arguments made by both sides of the legalization debate. Chapters 5, 6, and 7 provide a description of the statements made by the professionals concerning the legalization of marijuana when asked how the new policies would affect them as they perform their jobs. An analysis of this information is the focus of the remaining chapters of the book. Here, the major trends and patterns in the responses from members of the different professions are shown as well as the differences among the different professions. These chapters seek to answer the question of how legalization will affect different jobs in the next few years. In the end, this book provides an understanding of some of the ways that marijuana legalization will impact different occupations.

Chapter Two

History and Current Laws

The laws and policies that define the legal status of marijuana across the United States have been redefined by public referendum or the state legislatures during the past few years. Marijuana is not new to the United States. It could be found in the colonies but there was little regulation of the plant, as it was not considered to be a hindrance. The first law to control marijuana use in the United States was passed in 1906, and since then, multiple regulations have been created to ban or limit use, growth, and distribution of the plant. This chapter provides a brief history of the policies created to restrict the use of marijuana and a description of the current federal policies.

ABOUT THE PLANT

Marijuana is the most commonly used illegal substance in the world.[1] Also known as weed, pot, Mary Jane, and cannabis, among other terms, it is a naturally occurring plant that contains psychoactive substances. When it is smoked, eaten, or otherwise ingested, it can produce an altered state in users, making them feel a "high" that can be described as a sense of euphoria. It is also thought to alleviate pain or the symptoms of a multitude of medical conditions including glaucoma, AIDS, and epilepsy. Marijuana is typically considered to be a "softer" drug as compared to substances such as cocaine, meth, or heroin, which are sometimes referred to as "hard" drugs.

There are an estimated four hundred cannabinoids in marijuana. The primary psychoactive chemical cannabinoid in marijuana—the active ingredient that makes people high—is delta-9-tetrahydrocannabinol, more commonly known as THC.[2] When a user ingests THC, the substance attaches to the cannabinoid receptors on the surface of the nerve cells that are found in the portion of the brain that affects a person's concentration, memory, and coordination.[3]

Another cannabinoid found in marijuana is cannabidiol, or CBD, which is attributed to the medical properties of the plant. When this cannabinoid is ingested, users do not experience the same feelings of being "high" as they do after using THC. CBD is said to help reduce inflammation, pain, high blood pressure, congestion, nausea, and a host of other medical symptoms. It is thought to help those suffering from schizophrenia, multiple sclerosis, Tourette's syndrome, and opioid addiction.

Most people think that there is only one kind of marijuana plant, but there are hundreds of subspecies of marijuana plants that each have their own characteristics. One main type is *Cannabis sativa*. This plant has long stalks and separated branches. Also known as hemp, this variety grows easily in many climates from Canada to England.[4] It is usually produced for its durable fiber and is often used for things like textiles, cords, ropes, and twine. The cloth manufactured with hemp can be used for clothing, blankets, and boat sails. Hemp seeds are often used as a source of food and oil.[5] This plant has only trace amounts of THC and does not make users "high" if ingested.

The second main type of marijuana is *Cannabis indica*, which is cultivated for its high THC content and intoxicating qualities. The THC is found in the flowers or buds on the plant, which are covered with tiny trichomes. The stems and stalks of the plant have no psychoactive ingredients. Users dry the leaves and flowering buds, which are then ingested to produce an altered state or to alleviate different medical symptoms.[6] The amount of THC in different plants can vary dramatically because unique strains have varying amounts of cannabinoids. The amount of THC in the plant can be affected by the location of the grow site, the weather, and even the time the plant is harvested.[7]

When this type of marijuana is ingested, the user will feel sensations that are referred to as being "high." If the user smokes the plant, the effects can be felt within minutes; if the marijuana is eaten (i.e., in cookies or candy), the effects can take longer to appear. When a person uses marijuana, the THC hooks onto a protein in the brain called cannabinoid receptor type 1, also known as CB1. The THC found in marijuana is biphasic, which means that the drug can have different effects in different people or at different times.

In low doses, marijuana can affect the user's senses and mood. The user may feel relaxed, elated, or blissful. Most users experience dilated pupils. They may also experience distortions in comprehension and visual perception, such as distance or colors. Some users report changes in their judgment and insight. A user may have dryness in the mouth, an increased pulse and blood pressure, sensitivity to the touch, an increased appetite and involuntary twitching. Some users feel moments of ecstasy while others report feeling nauseous. Marijuana may impact memory and a user's ability to learn new things. Users also experience difficulty in motor control and may stumble or feel uncoordinated. A well-known effect is an increase in appetite, referred to as the "munchies."

If users ingest a large dose of marijuana, they may experience delirium, nervousness, hallucinations, paranoia, and feelings of being out of control. Others experience anxiety, symptoms of panic attacks, extreme nausea and vomiting, or psychotic reactions. Some report periods of amnesia while using marijuana. This can increase the chance that a user will engage in violent behaviors.[8]

The effects of marijuana use are partly influenced by one's state of mind and also by the environment or setting in which the individual is in. This state of being "high" or "stoned" can last a few hours after ingesting the product.[9] Because the THC is stored in the body's lipophilic tissue (fat cells), it remains in a user's bloodstream for days. Trace amounts of THC are released slowly into the body, but the amounts are so small that the user does not feel any effects.

Another form of marijuana is called hashish, or hash. It is compressed resin that is produced when cannabinoids are extracted from the leaves and flowers of the marijuana plant. Hash is most often produced in northern Africa or Asia. It can be eaten but is more often smoked in a pipe or bong. Another product, hash oil, is the end result of extracting the THC through a chemical process. It has a high content of THC and is often found in marijuana dispensaries. Some people choose to mix hash oil with different types of oil for use in cooking and making edibles.

There are indications that the potency of marijuana has increased in recent years. Growers have learned better methods of producing marijuana and have created new strains of the plant with higher levels of THC. It has been reported that the marijuana now being sold legally in Colorado has about three times as much THC as the marijuana that previously was sold on the street.[10] This change has potentially dangerous effects. Users may get a more intense effect from using the drug than in the past, possibly increasing the risk of adverse effects (paranoia, anxiety). The higher potency could be dangerous to inexperienced users who may unwittingly ingest more than they should.[11] At the same time, as marijuana growers have made the strains more potent, they have also reduced the amount of cannabidiol (CBD) in the plant, which is the component that may have medical benefits.[12] It should be noted that some plants are genetically engineered to have more CBD than THC. Some different strains of marijuana are listed in box 2.1.

There are many ways to ingest marijuana. The method most widely used is smoking, which allows the cannabinoids to be absorbed quickly into the bloodstream. Marijuana can also be eaten in food products, including cookies, brownies, soda, or tea. It is also used in salads and infused into oils. Marijuana that is ingested orally is referred to as an edible. Some people use marijuana in lotions or salves.

When Colorado and Washington State legalized recreational marijuana, there were no packaging or labelling requirements for edible products. Many of the edibles were sold in bright packages that looked like any other candy product. As a result, some people did not recognize the possible risk the product posed and ate too much. Emergency room personnel reported an increase in visits by people who ingested more than they should have. More young children were admitted to the hospital after mistakenly eating edibles.[13] There was also an increase in calls to poison control centers.

As a result, state legislatures in Colorado, Alaska, Oregon, and Washington passed new laws requiring manufacturers to create packaging for edibles that reflect the product's contents. In Colorado, Washington, and Oregon, officials created a universal symbol that must be applied to the labels of edible marijuana products. In Oregon and Colorado, the new laws require that users be informed if pesticides were used on the product. Manufacturers in Colorado and Oregon must include a nutrition facts

TEXTBOX 2.1. STRAINS OF MARIJUANA

Black Beauty: can be used to increase appetite or for posttraumatic stress disorder; can help users feel relaxed, alert, and sociable

White Widow: a popular type of marijuana

Big Bud: winner of the Cannabis Cup

Ice: a newer strain of marijuana that is highly crystalline and produces a strong high

Jack Herrer: considered to be the world's best marijuana

Master Kush: two-time winner of the Cannabis Cup

Papaya: has a tropical taste; makes users feel lethargic

Skunk: one of the most widely used strains worldwide; smells "skunky"

Super Glue: has woodsy, earth tones; makes users feel giggly

Buddha's Sister: helps with arthritis and Crohn's disease

Grape Krush: provides a warm and relaxing sensation

Power Plant: contains high levels of THC, which produces a strong high

Atomical Haze: known to be useful for reducing stress

Girl Scout Cookies: an extremely potent variety

*Willie Nelso*n: recommended for people suffering from depression and anxiety

Source: "Types of Marijuana," www.marijuana-picture.com/types_ of_marijuana_gallery_4.html; "Strains," www.marijuana.com/ strains.

panel on the packaging of all edible products, and in Alaska and Oregon, manufacturers are required to report how much THC is included in a single serving of the product. The legislation in all of these states requires that the packaging not be made attractive for children in order to deter them from unintentionally eating the product.[14]

Marijuana remains in the body after use and can be detected in a user for many days. If the person uses marijuana often or uses a lot of it, he or she can test positive for weeks after use. THC can also remain in a person's hair for months. However, testing hair can be a lengthy and expensive process.[15]

It is currently illegal to grow, distribute, possess, or use marijuana in the United States under federal law. The Controlled Substances Act passed in 1970 categorizes marijuana as a Schedule 1 drug, meaning that it has no medical benefits and a high risk of abuse. Many states allow marijuana use for medical or recreational reasons. In those states where marijuana remains illegal, the punishment for possessing it includes fines, imprisonment, and forfeiture of property. However, it was not always this way. In the section that follows, we see that marijuana has a long history in the United States and around the world.

HISTORY OF MARIJUANA USE

Marijuana has been used for thousands of years for many purposes. It has been used as a medicine, food, fiber, and, of course, as a recreational substance. The use of marijuana probably began in China, where the seeds were used as a food source. In fact, for thousands of years, marijuana was the second or third most prominent agricultural food source in that country.[16] Marijuana was also used in early Chinese culture for its strong fibers to make rope and fabric and to make hemp paper.[17]

The Chinese also relied on the medicinal qualities of the plant. The writings of Emperor Shen Nung in 2737 BC mention marijuana,[18] and a medical text from 1578 AD describes medical purposes for marijuana use. In this text, marijuana is described as a treatment for hundreds of medical problems including diarrhea, vomiting, parasitic infections, rheumatism, malaria, gout, and absentmindedness.[19]

Marijuana was found not only in China but in other cultures as well. The Hindus and Nihang Sikhs from India and Nepal were known to have consumed the plant, and the ancient Assyrians may have used marijuana in religious ceremonies.[20] Greeks relied on marijuana to relieve swelling, earaches, and edema, and others relied on it to stop nosebleeds and dress wounds on their horses.[21] Marijuana was used by ancient Jews, early Christians, and early Sufi Muslims.[22] Evidence indicates that marijuana was used in Egypt to treat gout, foot pain, eye problems, and hemorrhoids.

Medical treatments using marijuana were common for snakebites, asthma, and dysentery in Africa in the fifteenth century,[23] and in Rome, a doctor in the army of Emperor Nero recommended marijuana for multiple ailments including earaches.[24]

Marijuana has a long history in the United States. In 1492, Christopher Columbus had marijuana on his ships that came to the new world. The ships reportedly carried enough to last the crew through the journey until they could plant more.[25] In Jamestown, the first permanent English settlement in America, the marijuana plant was grown for its fiber content and became a major commercial crop along with tobacco. It became an essential part of Jamestown's economy, so that in 1619, Virginia made it a law that colonists grow hemp. Those who grew it were rewarded with coins, and those who did not faced possible penalties.[26]

Many of the early U.S. presidents grew marijuana. George Washington grew the plant for its hemp in 1765 and continued to do so for about thirty years. Some reports suggest that he grew it for medicinal reasons but also for its psychoactive qualities.[27] John Adams and Thomas Jefferson, the second and third presidents of the new country, also grew marijuana for its fiber. It is believed that Jefferson grew marijuana in a portion of his private garden, but there is no evidence that he smoked it or any other substance.[28] More about this is in box 2.2.

The use of marijuana in the United States grew in the late 1880s. A variety of medicines that included marijuana were readily available in pharmacies and drugstores.[29] It was used commonly to treat maladies such as skin inflammation and rashes, rabies, and tetanus.[30] The U.S. dispensatory in 1854 listed multiple uses for marijuana, including gout, tetanus, cholera, convulsions, depression, and insanity. The *United States Pharmacopeia* from 1850 to 1942 suggested that marijuana be used to assist with nausea, rheumatism, and for contractions during labor and delivery.[31]

In the early 1900s, the outlook on marijuana began to change. Many states started to pass laws banning the use of marijuana. The first state to do so was Massachusetts in 1911. In 1913, Maine, Wyoming, and Indiana banned use of the plant, followed by New York City in 1914. Utah and Vermont followed suit in 1915, with Colorado and Nevada banning it in 1917.[32]

TEXTBOX 2.2.   THE FOUNDING FATHERS AND MARIJUANA

It is a common misperception that founding fathers George Washington, Thomas Jefferson, James Madison, and Ben Franklin grew and used marijuana for recreation and enjoyment. It is likely that the founding fathers grew *Cannabis sativa*, the variety of marijuana also known as hemp. It has very little THC and is not used to get high. In colonial America, hemp was considered to be a valuable product that had the potential to be extremely profitable. At that time, hemp was a crop grown for the fibrous nature of the product. It was used to make rope and canvas products for ships, linen cloth for fabric, and pulp for paper. In the early 1600s, every farmer in Virginia was required to grow hemp. It was then used as legal tender in that state and in Pennsylvania and Maryland.

The founding fathers each spoke about the benefits of hemp. George Washington grew hemp on his farmlands. Ben Franklin used hemp fibers to make paper in his paper mill. But it is unlikely that Washington and Jefferson grew hemp as a way to get high or for recreational reasons. If the founding fathers did smoke hemp, they likely didn't get high from it.

Source: "Busting Some Myths about the Founding Fathers and Marijuana." The National Constitution Center. https://constitution-center.org/blog/busting-some-myths-about-the-founding-fathers-and-marijuana.

MEDICAL MARIJUANA

Marijuana has been used for centuries for medical purposes. In 1839, a professor of chemistry and surgeon in India published a study on the effects of marijuana for treating diseases. He relied on case studies of people who were suffering from diseases such as rheumatism, cholera, and tetanus and who found relief through the use of marijuana. Moreover, there were no serious side effects. He was able to convince people that marijuana could be an effective medical treatment option.[33]

Today, marijuana is reported to help with a variety of symptoms, including nausea, pain, and headaches. A 2014 survey of doctors found that more than two-thirds agreed that marijuana should be an option for their patients.[34] In 2017, the National Academy of Medicine (NAM) reported that there was considerable evidence that marijuana could be an effective treatment for patients who suffer from nausea or chronic pain.[35] Some of the reasons patients use medical marijuana are listed in box 2.3.

Synthetic marijuana, or Marinol, is sometimes used to increase a patient's appetite or to reduce nausea. Many people report that it does not work as well as smoking marijuana. It is also reported to cause serious side effects in some users, such as depression, paranoia, hallucinations, and psychosis.[36]

TEXTBOX 2.3. AILMENTS TREATED WITH MARIJUANA

AIDS (wasting syndrome)
alcohol withdrawal
Alzheimer's disease
anorexia
cancer
Crohn's disease
depression
diabetes
fibromyalgia
glaucoma
high blood pressure
insomnia
migraines
pain
seizures

FEDERAL LAWS ON MARIJUANA

Marijuana was legal and commonly used through the nineteenth century as a pain reliever and remained as such until the invention of aspirin. It was used in some patent medicines, but most of those contained cocaine or opium. The earliest ban on the sale of marijuana was in 1906 when the Pure Food and Drug Act was passed in Congress and signed into law by President Roosevelt. The law created the Food and Drug Administration (FDA), which was given the task of regulating the safety of all foods and drugs that would be consumed by humans. Provisions in the law also limited the sale of some drugs without a prescription from a physician and required specific labelling for any drug with the potential to be habit forming.[37] This meant that any product that contained alcohol, marijuana, opium, cocaine, or any other addictive substance had to indicate that to the consumer. In addition, the law limited marijuana use for research studies overseen by the FDA and outlawed importation of the drug from Mexico not intended for medical purposes.[38]

In 1914, Congress passed the Harrison Act as a way to regulate the importation and use of opium. The law also banned the buying and selling of marijuana for nonmedicinal purposes. It did not prohibit the use of marijuana for medical reasons, and people continued to use it for that.[39]

During the 1920s, when Prohibition outlawed the use of alcohol, marijuana became more popular.[40] Its use was linked with jazz musicians and those in show business in New Orleans[41] and with immigrant Mexican workers who came to the United States seeking jobs.[42] At this point, marijuana was not used by most Americans. Marijuana use by Mexicans became a concern to many Americans who believed that "all Mexicans are crazy, and this stuff is what makes them crazy."[43] It was even more dangerous because it was thought that using marijuana gave users "superhuman strength and turned them into bloodthirsty murderers."[44]

In the 1930s, Harry Anslinger, the head of the U.S. Federal Bureau of Narcotics (part of the Department of the Treasury), was vehemently opposed to the use of marijuana.[45] To Anslinger, marijuana was a powerfully addictive and harmful drug, and users were often known to use harder drugs. It was reported that Anslinger, as a way to influence the public's attitudes toward marijuana, would "fabricate horror stories" about marijuana use and the violent crime that users would commit after using it.[46]

Anslinger often blamed Mexicans for bringing the drug into the United States and then for committing crimes after using it. He said "marijuana was introduced into the United States from Mexico and swept across America with incredible speed."[47] Further, "smoking marijuana inspired blacks and Hispanics to commit rape and engage in other acts of uninhibited violence."[48] Anslinger reported that a man from Florida smoked marijuana then used an axe to kill his family.[49]

Anslinger successfully waged a public "misinformation campaign" against marijuana in which he portrayed it as causing insanity and violence.[50] Because of his antimarijuana campaign, most people believed that those who used marijuana would become violent criminals. He successfully influenced federal policies and public opinion to regard marijuana as an evil drug and was able to convince many states to pass laws to outlaw the use of the plant.[51] Many other states disagreed with Anslinger and refused to take part. They considered Anslinger to be interfering in their affairs. More on Harry Anslinger is provided in box 2.4.

Because of Anslinger's actions, Congress passed the Marijuana Tax Act of 1937, and President Roosevelt signed it into law. This new law did not ban marijuana use but imposed new laws that restricted its use. Under the law, anyone who bought, sold, or grew marijuana had to file paperwork with the federal government and buy a stamp from the Department of the Treasury. The cost of the stamp varied. Producers or medical professionals paid $1 per year; those who were not in the medical field paid $5; and anyone who imported or manufactured the drug paid $24. Those who were caught growing or possessing marijuana without the stamp faced criminal penalties that included a $2,000 fine and up to five years in prison.[52]

Interestingly, the Treasury did not issue any stamps. Since people were unable to purchase the stamp, people who grew, sold, or possessed marijuana were breaking the law.

Additionally, the regulations included in the law made it difficult if not impossible for physicians to prescribe marijuana to patients. Most doctors decided it was safer not to prescribe marijuana to patients and to rely on other drugs instead. In essence, the Marijuana Tax Act put a halt to the medical use of marijuana in the United States at that time.[53] Moreover, many growers found it too expensive to grow the plant legally. In the long run, the new law caused marijuana products to be grown and

TEXTBOX 2.4.   HARRY ANSLINGER (1892–1975)

Harry Anslinger was born in Altoona, Pennsylvania. Early in his law enforcement career, Anslinger was hired to investigate arson cases and to gather statistics. During World War I, Anslinger became an overseer of government contracts. He remained in Europe at the end of the war to investigate drugs being smuggled from Germany into the United States. This led him to the Bahamas to study the illegal transportation of rum, where he convinced officials to improve their record keeping of rum shipments. This was such a success that Anslinger was appointed to serve in the Prohibition Unit in the United States as the chief of the Foreign Control section, later becoming the assistant commissioner of prohibition. He fought alcohol smuggling by increasing punishments for violators. At the end of Prohibition, Anslinger became the chief of the Federal Bureau of Narcotics, serving in that position from 1930 to 1962. He often described the dangers of drug use, seeking tougher punishments for sellers and users. He focused attention on publicizing the dangers of drugs and fought to get major legislation passed by Congress to increase the criminalization of marijuana and to establish mandatory minimum sentences for drug offenders and traffickers. Anslinger retired in 1962 but continued the fight against drugs by becoming the U.S. representative to the United Nations Narcotics Commission. He passed away in 1975 at the age of eighty-three.

Source: Frydl, Kathleen J. (2013). *The Drug Wars in America, 1940–1973*. Cambridge: Cambridge University Press.

sold illegally.[54] As an interesting note, the Marijuana Tax Act was ruled unconstitutional by the U.S. Supreme Court in 1969 in the case of *Leary v. United States* (see box 2.5).

In 1944, a report called "The Marihuana Problem in the City of New York" was published. The document, prepared by the New York Academy of Medicine, was more widely referred to as the LaGuardia Committee Report after the mayor of New York, Fiorello LaGuardia. The

TEXTBOX 2.5. COURT DECISION
FROM LEARY (395 U.S. 6 [1969])

In December 1965, Timothy Leary was travelling from New York to Mexico with his daughter, son, and two others. They were denied entry into Mexico and chose to return to the United States via the International Bridge to Texas. A customs officer found some marijuana in the car and in the daughter's possession. Leary was convicted under the Marijuana Tax Act because he had knowingly facilitated the transportation and concealment of marijuana without paying the transfer tax required by the Marijuana Tax Act. Leary claimed that his conviction under the Marijuana Tax Act violated his privilege against self-incrimination.

The court decided that the law denied the defendant due process of law, a violation of the Fifth Amendment. They found that the Marijuana Tax Act compelled Leary to expose himself to a "real and appreciable" risk of self-incrimination and required him to identify himself not only as a transferee of marijuana but as a transferee who had not registered and paid the tax.

The court reversed Leary's conviction, noting that "nothing in what we hold today implies any constitutional disability in Congress to deal with the marijuana traffic by other means." Not long after, the Marijuana Tax Act was repealed by members of Congress when they passed a new law, the Comprehensive Drug Abuse Prevention and Control Act, in 1970.

mayor, unsure whether marijuana caused crime and mayhem, appointed a group of experts to study the social, medical, and psychological effects of marijuana use on the city. The committee members studied seventy-seven inmates who all admitted to being long-term users of marijuana. The members concluded that use of marijuana does not lead to addiction, violent or antisocial behavior, uncontrollable sexual urges, nor to the use of other drugs. They also concluded that most school-aged children did not use marijuana, nor did most juvenile offenders, and that marijuana use did not result in changes to a person's personality. LaGuardia himself wrote that the drug should not be decriminalized but noted that more research should be done on the possible use of marijuana to treat those addicted to narcotics.[55]

Anslinger was furious about the report and sought to discredit it. He destroyed every copy he could find. He sought to disgrace those who disagreed with him. Many of his adversaries were in the entertainment industry and feared potential repercussions of Anslinger's attacks. To prevent this, they allowed Anslinger to review movie scripts that referenced drug use, and he banned any that he considered to be offensive.

More restrictions on marijuana were established in 1951, when Congress passed the Boggs Act, signed into law by President Truman.[56] This new law increased the mandatory minimum sentences for people who imported marijuana into the United States. It also established sentences for anyone who received, concealed, bought, sold, transported, or trafficked in marijuana. Those convicted faced fines of up to $2,000 and prison terms of two to five years. For a second offense, the possible sentence increased to five to ten years, and offenders faced ten to twenty years for a third offense. Additionally, the Boggs Act established that marijuana had no therapeutic uses so it was no longer was considered to be a medicine.[57]

Four years later, in 1956, Congress instituted further limits on marijuana with the Narcotic Control Act of 1956. This new law established increased penalties for those who produced, distributed, or used marijuana. There was a mandatory two- to ten-year prison term for a person convicted of possession of marijuana. If the offense was serious enough, the offender could be sentenced to death.[58] Some states added additional penalties. In Missouri, for example, a person convicted of a second offense for marijuana possession could be sentenced to a life term in prison.

Even though marijuana was illegal in many states and by the federal government, marijuana was still used by a significant number of people.[59] In the 1960s, the plant reemerged as a fashionable drug among white middle-class youth who saw it as a way to rebel against authority and reject society's value system.[60] Veterans returning from Vietnam used it to deal with injuries and posttraumatic stress disorder. It is no surprise that growing public concern about the drug resulted.

In April 1968, President Johnson created a new agency called the Bureau of Narcotics and Dangerous Drugs, which spotlighted illicit drug and narcotic use in the United States. More action to ban drugs occurred during the Nixon administration. A major antinarcotics law, the Comprehensive Drug Abuse Prevention and Control Act, sometimes known as the Controlled Substances Act (CSA), was passed in 1970. The intent of the law was regulating the legal drug industry while at the same time limiting the transportation and distribution of illegal drugs in the United States. Provisions in the law abolished mandatory minimum sentences for marijuana offenses and also reduced possible penalties for conviction of marijuana possession.

The law created five "schedules" or classifications of drugs, which were based on whether the drugs had recognized medical benefits to patients and also on their potential for abuse and addiction. All drugs placed in Schedule 1 were deemed to have no recognized medical value and a high potential for abuse and addiction. Examples of Schedule 1 drugs include heroin, LSD, and hashish. Those in Schedule 2 had some limited or accepted medical purpose, along with a high potential for abuse, such as barbiturates and amphetamines (morphine and cocaine). All Schedule 3 drugs had recognized medical uses and high potential for abuse, including codeine. Drugs identified in Schedule 4 had a lower potential to cause psychological dependence and abuse than those in Schedule 1, 2, and 3 and currently acceptable medical uses. Those drugs placed in Schedule 5 had an accepted medical use but a low potential for abuse. Marijuana was placed into Schedule 1, indicating that it has no medical value and a high potential of abuse. The drug schedules are outlined in more detail in box 2.6.

Congress did not pass any further significant drug control legislation until the Anti-Drug Abuse acts of 1986 and 1988, which became part of President Reagan's War on Drugs. Among other things, the laws increased minimum penalties for the possession or sale of large amounts of marijuana. The sentence offenders received for violating the law depended in part on the amount of drug they possessed. A person in possession of one hundred marijuana plants received the same sentence as a person who possessed 100 grams of heroin. Serious offenders could face up to life in prison and a $10 million fine. Penalties doubled for offenders who sold drugs to minors or who used minors to sell drugs.

The 1988 bill not only increased penalties for drug law violations, but it created grants to help schools and communities pay for educational

TEXTBOX 2.6.   DRUG SCHEDULES

Schedule 1 drugs, substances, or chemicals are defined as drugs with no currently accepted medical use and a high potential for abuse. Some examples of Schedule 1 drugs are heroin, lysergic acid diethylamide (LSD), marijuana (cannabis), ecstasy, methaqualone, and peyote.

Schedule 2 drugs, substances, or chemicals are defined as drugs with a high potential for abuse, with use potentially leading to severe psychological or physical dependence. These drugs are also considered dangerous. Some examples of Schedule 2 drugs are combination products with less than 15 milligrams of hydrocodone per dosage unit (Vicodin), cocaine, methamphetamine, methadone, hydromorphone (Dilaudid), meperidine (Demerol), oxycodone (OxyContin), fentanyl, Dexedrine, Adderall, and Ritalin.

Schedule 3 drugs, substances, or chemicals are defined as drugs with a moderate to low potential for physical and psychological dependence. Abuse potential for Schedule 3 drugs is less than Schedule 1 and Schedule 2 drugs but more than Schedule 4. Some examples of Schedule 3 drugs are products containing less than 90 milligrams of codeine per dosage unit (Tylenol with codeine), ketamine, anabolic steroids, and testosterone.

Schedule 4 drugs, substances, or chemicals are defined as drugs with a low potential for abuse and a low risk of dependence. Some examples of Schedule 4 drugs are Xanax, Soma, Darvon, Darvocet, Valium, Ativan, Ambien, and Tramadol.

Schedule 5 drugs, substances, or chemicals are defined as drugs with lower potential for abuse than Schedule 4 and consist of preparations containing limited quantities of certain narcotics. Schedule 5 drugs are generally used for antidiarrheal, antitussive, and analgesic purposes. Some examples of Schedule 5 drugs are cough preparations with less than 200 milligrams of codeine per 100 milliliters (Robitussin AC), Lomotil, Motofen, Lyrica, and Parepectolin.

Source: "Drug Scheduling." Drug Enforcement Administration. www.dea.gov/druginfo/ds.shtml.

programs aimed at deterring drug use and funding treatment programs. In addition, the federal government created a new position, the "drug czar," who was tasked with overseeing the nation's antidrug policies.

Current Federal Marijuana Policy

At this point, the laws regulating marijuana are confusing. There are federal, state, and even some local laws regulating marijuana. At the federal level, there has been limited legislative action on marijuana since the 1970 CSA was passed. Proposals have been introduced into Congress that would allow for federal laws permitting medical marijuana. One of those proposals, from Representative Barney Frank (D-MA), included provisions to eliminate federal restrictions on marijuana and allow states to decide. Despite support from many states, the bill did not pass Congress. Box 2.7 gives more examples of bills proposed in Congress concerning marijuana.

Individual states and cities that opposed the restrictions on marijuana set forth in the CSA decided to pass laws that allowed for marijuana use. San Francisco passed a ballot initiative in November 1991 that required state officials and the California Medical Association to list marijuana as an available medicine for residents of that state. The initiative also prohibited sanctioning physicians who recommended marijuana to their patients. The initiative, called Proposition B, was passed by voters with 79 percent of the vote.

Voters in the entire state of California chose to support Proposition 215, which was on the ballot in 1996 (see box 2.8). Also called the Compassionate Use Act, the proposal gave patients and their caregivers the right to possess and cultivate marijuana as a treatment for a variety of medical disorders including AIDS, cancer, and muscular spasticity. Moreover, doctors could not be sanctioned for recommending that patients use the plant.[61] When Proposition 215 passed, California became the first state to legalize medical marijuana.

Other states followed California's lead and passed legislation to allow residents to use marijuana for medical reasons. In November 1999, voters in Maine passed a proposal that allowed marijuana for medical uses, along with provisions for possession and cultivation. In June 2000, Hawaii legislators did the same, and in 2000, laws passed in Nevada and Colorado.

TEXTBOX 2.7. SELECTED MARIJUANA-RELATED BILLS PROPOSED IN CONGRESS

H.R. 4467/S. 2504, 114th Congress (2015–2016): Marijuana Advertising in Legal States Act of 2016 (MAILS Act) proposed to modify the Controlled Substances Act (CSA). Under the CSA, it is illegal to place an ad in a newspaper, magazine, or other similar source as a way to receive, buy, or distribute a Schedule 1 controlled substance such as marijuana. Under the proposed law, this advertising prohibition would not apply to ads for marijuana-related activities that abide state law.

S. 683, 114th Congress (2015–2016): Compassionate Access, Research Expansion, and Respect States Act of 2015 (CARERS Act of 2015) would amend the CSA so that any provisions related to the control and enforcement of the laws pertaining to marijuana in the CSA shall not apply to those who are in compliance with state laws. It also transfers marijuana from a Schedule 1 to a Schedule 2 drug.

H.R. 1635, 113th Congress (2013–2014): National Commission on Federal Marijuana Policy Act of 2013 proposed the creation of a new agency called the National Commission on Federal Marijuana Policy, which would review all existing federal policies related to marijuana in light of the increasing number of states in which marijuana is now permitted for medical or recreational use.

H.R. 2306, 112th Congress (2011–2012): Ending Federal Marijuana Prohibition Act of 2011 proposed to amend the CSA to remove marijuana from Schedule 1 classification.

H. Res. 372, 105th Congress (1997–1998): Declared that the House of Representatives opposed the legalization of marijuana for medical reasons. The bill also recommended that state initiatives to legalize marijuana for medical reasons be stopped. In addition, the bill mandated that the attorney general provide members of the House Judiciary Committee information concerning the total amount of marijuana eradicated in the United States from 1992 through 1997 and provide information on the annual number of people arrested and prosecuted for violation of federal marijuana laws.

TEXTBOX 2.8. TEXT OF
CALIFORNIA'S PROPOSITION 215 INITIATIVE

Section 1. Section 11362.5 is added to the California Health and Safety Code, to read:

11362.5. (a) This section shall be known and may be cited as the Compassionate Use Act of 1996.

(b) (1) The people of the State of California hereby find and declare that the purposes of the Compassionate Use Act of 1996 are as follows:

(A) To ensure that seriously ill Californians have the right to obtain and use marijuana for medical purposes where that medical use is deemed appropriate and has been recommended by a physician who has determined that the person's health would benefit from the use of marijuana in the treatment of cancer, anorexia, AIDS, chronic pain, spasticity, glaucoma, arthritis, migraine, or any other illness for which marijuana provides relief.

(B) To ensure that patients and their primary caregivers who obtain and use marijuana for medical purposes upon the recommendation of a physician are not subject to criminal prosecution or sanction.

(C) To encourage the federal and state governments to implement a plan for the safe and affordable distribution of marijuana to all patients in medical need of marijuana.

(2) Nothing in this act shall be construed to supersede legislation prohibiting persons from engaging in conduct that endangers others, nor to condone the diversion of marijuana for nonmedical purposes.

(c) Notwithstanding any other provision of law, no physician in this state shall be punished, or denied any right or privilege, for having recommended marijuana to a patient for medical purposes.

(d) Section 11357, relating to the possession of marijuana, and Section 11358, relating to the cultivation of marijuana, shall not apply to a patient, or to a patient's primary caregiver, who possesses or cultivates marijuana for the personal medical purposes of the patient upon the written or oral recommendation or approval of a physician.

(e) For the purposes of this section, primary caregiver means the individual designated by the person exempted under this act who has consistently assumed responsibility for the housing, health or safety of that person.

Sec. 2. If any provision of this measure or the application thereof to any person or circumstance is held invalid, that invalidity shall not affect other provisions or applications of the measure which can be given effect without the invalid provision or application, and to this end the provisions of this measure are severable.

The state legislatures in Vermont and Montana changed their laws to allow for medical marijuana use in 2004.[62] This was followed by Rhode Island in 2006, New Mexico in 2007, and Michigan in 2008. In addition, Alaska, Colorado, Oregon, and Washington have passed laws that permit residents to use marijuana for recreational purposes.

Although these state laws permit cultivation, possession, and use of marijuana for either medical or recreational purposes, these acts remain illegal under federal law. Under the CSA, marijuana remains a Schedule 1 drug. That means it has no recognized medical benefits and a high potential for addiction and abuse. A person who imports, grows, cultivates, distributes, or uses the substance may be protected under state laws but not federal laws. Other drugs in this category include heroin and cocaine. A person using any of these substances could be charged with a federal crime even if the state permits it.

The policy implications remain unclear. In the United States, the federal government, particularly Congress, has the power to pass laws to regulate people's behavior. The U.S. Constitution describes the types of laws that Congress can pass and the types that the states can pass. If the Constitution is silent on a particular subject, it is delegated to the states. The topics of crime control and drugs are not defined by the Constitution as areas in which the federal government can make laws. Therefore, laws that define crimes and sanctions should be passed by the states.

However, in the past sixty years or so, the federal government has passed numerous laws creating federal crimes, many regulating illicit drugs. This process of increased federal action in the area of crime has been called the "federalization of crime." In essence, crime and drugs have moved from being an issue defined by states to an issue also defined by federal laws.

It should also be noted that in situations in which a state has created a law that conflicts with an existing federal law, the federal law supersedes the state law. This is called the Supremacy Clause. In the case of marijuana, many states have passed laws to regulate who can possess, use, manufacture, and transport the plant. However, these laws conflict with the federal CSA. In this case, federal law should prevail, and the new state laws on marijuana may be invalid.[63]

Memos

Attempting to address some of the confusion regarding the clash between the federal and state laws related to marijuana use, the Department of Justice issued a series of memos that outlined the status of federal enforcement efforts. The first of the memos was released in October 2009 by the U.S. attorney general at that time, Eric Holder. The memo, written by David Ogden, the deputy attorney general, became known as the Ogden memo (see box 2.9). In it, officials made it clear that Drug Enforcement Administration (DEA) agents would not raid marijuana dispensaries in states that had passed laws to allow for marijuana use. As written in the memo, "As a general matter, pursuit of [federal law enforcement] priorities should not focus federal resources . . . on individuals whose actions are in clear and unambiguous compliance with existing state laws providing for the medical use of marijuana."[64] For most people, this memo seemed to indicate that federal law enforcement would not carry out raids on dispensaries if the organizations were abiding by state laws.

Another memo was released in 2011 that seemed, in many ways, to reverse this policy. This memo became widely referred to as the Cole memo because it was written by James Cole, then the deputy attorney general. Cole instructed all federal law enforcement officials (including DEA agents) to put medical marijuana dispensaries at the top of their priority lists when enforcing federal laws on marijuana. A clause in the memo states, "persons who are in the business of cultivating, selling or distributing marijuana, and those who knowingly facilitate such activities, are in violation of the Controlled Substances Act, regardless of state law."[65]

TEXTBOX 2.9. 2009 OGDEN MEMO

U.S. Department of Justice
Office of the Deputy Attorney General
MEMORANDUM
FOR SELECTED UNITED STATES ATTORNEYS
FROM: David W. Ogden, Deputy Attorney General
SUBJECT: Investigations and Prosecutions in States Authorizing the Medical Use of Marijuana

This memorandum provides clarification and guidance to federal prosecutors in States that have enacted laws authorizing the medical use of marijuana. These laws vary in their substantive provisions and in the extent of state regulatory oversight, both among the enacting States and among local jurisdictions within those States. Rather than developing different guidelines for every possible variant of state and local law, this memorandum provides uniform guidance to focus federal investigations and prosecutions in these States on core federal enforcement priorities.

The Department of Justice is committed to the enforcement of the Controlled Substances Act in all States. Congress has determined that marijuana is a dangerous drug, and the illegal distribution and sale of marijuana is a serious crime and provides a significant source of revenue to large-scale criminal enterprises, gangs, and cartels. One timely example underscores the importance of our efforts to prosecute significant marijuana traffickers: marijuana distribution in the United States remains the single largest source of revenue for the Mexican cartels.

The Department is also committed to making efficient and rational use of its limited investigative and prosecutorial resources. In general, United States Attorneys are vested with "plenary authority with regard to federal criminal matters" within their districts. USAM 9-2.001. In exercising this authority, United States Attorneys are "invested by statute and delegation from the Attorney General with the broadest discretion in the exercise of such authority." *Id.* This authority should, of course, be exercised consistent with Department priorities and guidance.

The prosecution of significant traffickers of illegal drugs, including marijuana, and the disruption of illegal drug manufacturing and trafficking networks continue to be a core priority in the Department's efforts against narcotics and dangerous drugs, and the Department's investigative and prosecutorial resources should be directed towards these objectives. As a general matter, pursuit of these priorities should not focus federal resources in your States on individuals whose actions are in clear and unambiguous compliance with existing state laws providing for the medical use of marijuana. For example, prosecution of individuals with cancer or other serious illnesses who use marijuana as part of a recommended treatment regimen consistent with applicable state law, or those caregivers in clear and unambiguous compliance with existing state law who provide such individuals with marijuana, is unlikely to be an efficient use of limited federal resources. On the other hand, prosecution of commercial enterprises that unlawfully market and sell marijuana for profit continues to be an enforcement priority of the Department. To be sure, claims of compliance with state or local law may mask operations inconsistent with the terms, conditions, or purposes of those laws, and federal law enforcement should not be deterred by such assertions when otherwise pursuing the Department's core enforcement priorities.

Typically, when any of the following characteristics is present, the conduct will not be in clear and unambiguous compliance with applicable state law and may indicate illegal drug trafficking activity of potential federal interest:

- unlawful possession or unlawful use of firearms;
- violence;
- sales to minors;
- financial and marketing activities inconsistent with the terms, conditions, or purposes of state law, including evidence of money laundering activity and/or financial gains or excessive amounts of cash inconsistent with purported compliance with state or local law;

- amounts of marijuana inconsistent with purported compliance with state or local law;
- illegal possession or sale of other controlled substances; or
- ties to other criminal enterprises.

Of course, no State can authorize violations of federal law, and the list of factors above is not intended to describe exhaustively when a federal prosecution may be warranted. Accordingly, in prosecutions under the Controlled Substances Act, federal prosecutors are not expected to charge, prove, or otherwise establish any state law violations. Indeed, this memorandum does not alter in any way the Department's authority to enforce federal law, including laws prohibiting the manufacture, production, distribution, possession, or use of marijuana on federal property. This guidance regarding resource allocation does not "legalize" marijuana or provide a legal defense to a violation of federal law, nor is it intended to create any privileges, benefits, or rights, substantive or procedural, enforceable by any individual, party or witness in any administrative, civil, or criminal matter. Nor does clear and unambiguous compliance with state law or the absence of one or all of the above factors create a legal defense to a violation of the Controlled Substances Act. Rather, this memorandum is intended solely as a guide to the exercise of investigative and prosecutorial discretion.

Finally, nothing herein precludes investigation or prosecution where there is a reasonable basis to believe that compliance with state law is being invoked as a pretext for the production or distribution of marijuana for purposes not authorized by state law. Nor does this guidance preclude investigation or prosecution, even when there is clear and unambiguous compliance with existing state law, in particular circumstances where investigation or prosecution otherwise serves important federal interests.

Your offices should continue to review marijuana cases for prosecution on a case-by-case basis, consistent with the guidance on resource allocation and federal priorities set forth herein, the consideration of requests for federal assistance from state and local law enforcement authorities, and the Principles of Federal Prosecution.

Further, the document also stated, "such persons are subject to federal enforcement action, including potential prosecution. State laws or local ordinances are not a defense to civil or criminal enforcement of federal law with respect to such conduct, including enforcement of the CSA."[66] See box 2.10 for the text of the Cole memo.

TEXTBOX 2.10. 2011 COLE MEMO

Over the last several months some of you have requested the Department's assistance in responding to inquiries from State and local governments seeking guidance about the Department's position on enforcement of the Controlled Substances Act (CSA) in jurisdictions that have under consideration, or have implemented, legislation that would sanction and regulate the commercial cultivation and distribution of marijuana purportedly for medical use. Some of these jurisdictions have considered approving the cultivation of large quantities of marijuana, or broadening the regulation and taxation of the substance. You may have seen letters responding to these inquiries by several United States Attorneys. Those letters are entirely consistent with the October 2009 memorandum issued by Deputy Attorney General David Ogden to federal prosecutors in States that have enacted laws authorizing the medical use of marijuana (the "Ogden Memo").

The Department of Justice is committed to the enforcement of the Controlled Substances Act in all States. Congress has determined that marijuana is a dangerous drug and that the illegal distribution and sale of marijuana is a serious crime that provides a significant source of revenue to large scale criminal enterprises, gangs, and cartels. The Ogden Memorandum provides guidance to you in deploying your resources to enforce the CSA as part of the exercise of the broad discretion you are given to address federal criminal matters within your districts.

A number of states have enacted some form of legislation relating to the medical use of marijuana. Accordingly, the Ogden Memo reiterated to you that prosecution of significant traffickers of illegal drugs, including marijuana, remains a core priority, but advised that it is likely not an efficient use of federal resources to focus enforcement efforts on individuals with cancer or other serious illnesses who use marijuana as part of a recommended treatment regimen consistent with applicable state law, or their caregivers. The term "caregiver" as used in the memorandum meant just that: individuals providing care to individuals with cancer or other serious illnesses, not commercial operations cultivating, selling, or distributing marijuana.

The Department's view of the efficient use of limited federal resources as articulated in the Ogden Memorandum has not changed. There has, however, been an increase in the scope of commercial cultivation, sale, distribution and use of marijuana for purported medical purposes. For example, within the past 12 months, several jurisdictions have considered or enacted legislation to authorize multiple large-scale, privately operated industrial marijuana cultivation centers. Some of these planned facilities have revenue projections of millions of dollars based on the planned cultivation of tens of thousands of cannabis plants.

The Ogden Memorandum was never intended to shield such activities from federal enforcement action and prosecution, even where those activities purport to comply with state law. Persons who are in the business of cultivating, selling or distributing marijuana, and those who knowingly facilitate such activities, are in violation of the Controlled Substances Act, regardless of state law. Consistent with resource constraints and the discretion you may exercise in your district, such persons are subject to federal enforcement action, including potential prosecution. State laws or local ordinances are not a defense to civil or criminal enforcement of federal law with respect to such conduct, including enforcement of the CSA. Those who engage in transactions involving the proceeds of such activity may also be in violation of federal money laundering statutes and other federal financial laws. The Department of Justice is tasked with enforcing existing federal criminal laws in all states, and enforcement of the CSA has long been and remains a core priority.

James Cole wrote another memo that was released in 2013. In this memo, there were eight factors that law enforcement personnel were told to consider when deciding to enforce federal charges against those involved in a marijuana-related business. These factors included how successful the business was at preventing the distribution of marijuana to minors; if they prevented profits from the sale of marijuana from being transferred to any criminal enterprises (i.e., cartels); if the transportation of marijuana from states where it is legal to other states could be prevented; the prevention of state-authorized marijuana activity from being used to conceal the trafficking of other illegal narcotic drugs; the prevention of possible violence and the use of firearms in the cultivation and distribution of marijuana; prevention of drugged driving and other adverse public health consequences linked to marijuana use; prevention of growing marijuana on public lands; and prevention of possessing marijuana or use on federal property. The memo informs readers that if marijuana dispensaries were abiding by the state law and were operating in accordance with these eight priorities, the government should allow them to operate without federal intervention. If the laws were not extensive enough to address these eight priorities, the federal government could enforce the law against them.[67]

Near the end of the memo, Cole included the following, often referred to as the "safety clause": "As with the Department's previous statements on this subject, this memorandum is intended solely as a guide to the exercise of investigative and prosecutorial discretion. This memorandum does not alter in any way the Department's authority to enforce federal law, including federal laws relating to marijuana, regardless of state law. Neither the guidance herein nor any state or local law provides a legal defense to a violation of federal law, including any civil or criminal violation of the CSA." This statement is simply a reminder to all involved that marijuana is illegal under federal law and that law can be enforced at any time, regardless of state policy.[68]

Many people who work in marijuana-related businesses made note of the fact that Cole, in the 2013 memo, did not address concerns about the lack of banking options. Many businesses were unable to open accounts for the businesses since their profits are, under federal law, illegal. As defined by the federal Anti-Money Laundering/Bank Secrecy Act, profits earned from the sale of marijuana could be labeled as money laundering.

If banks accepted money from these businesses, bank officials could also be charged federally and possibly lose their operating license. Without a banking option available to them, many marijuana businesses rely only on cash, resulting in large amounts of cash in their stores.

To address this problem, another memo was issued on February 14, 2014, by the Department of the Treasury's Financial Crimes Enforcement Network. The "Banking Memo," as it came to be called, provided banking officials with guidance on how they could facilitate banking for those involved in a marijuana-related business. The memo was intended to give bank officials in states where marijuana was legalized some direction regarding the legalities of banking with these businesses; it also provided them with some assurances that they would not be charged by the federal government for violating the Bank Secrecy Act. It was thought that once banking officials were satisfied that they would not be charged, more cash proceeds would end up in banks as opposed to safes in the stores. Moreover, there would be better record keeping on the sales of marijuana for tax purposes.[69]

One final memo was issued by Attorney General Holder in February 2015 providing evidence that federal prosecutors were not basing their sentences on mandatory minimum sentences when punishing offenders found guilty of marijuana offenses. In the memo it was pointed out that many offenders received lower sentences for their offenses than what was in the guidelines. This information was proof that federal officials were allowing marijuana businesses to operate without federal interference. This was well-received news from those involved in marijuana-related businesses, providing some relief that they were free to continue operating.[70]

The fears of marijuana business owners were also addressed by members of Congress, who passed the Rohrabacher-Farr bill, which limited federal action toward marijuana businesses. The bill forbade the use of federal funds to prevent states from implementing their marijuana laws. Originally passed in December 2014, the bill was reauthorized a year later in December 2015 with bipartisan support. According to the law, DEA agents were not permitted to use federal funds from the Justice Department to pay for raids on medical marijuana dispensaries in states where it was legal. The amendment was originally set to expire on September 30, 2017, but it was added as an amendment to a short-term spending bill that was signed in September 2018. This amendment renewed it through December 2018. If, in the future, the amendment is not again renewed, DEA agents could begin carrying out raids on marijuana dispensaries, even if state laws permit them to operate.

In January 2018, attorney general of the United States, Jeff Sessions, announced that the Trump administration was reversing the lenient policies of the Obama administration. The new policies gave local prosecutors the power to decide whether to prosecute marijuana cultivators, distributors, sellers, or users.

STATE LAWS ON MARIJUANA

For many years, cities and states have passed their own laws on marijuana. For example, in 1972, Ann Arbor, Michigan, chose to remove marijuana possession from the criminal code, making that act a minor offense, the equivalent to a parking ticket. Oregon followed suit, and in 1973 passed a law that decriminalized marijuana. A study on marijuana use in that state following the new law found that there was no apparent increase in the number of people who used marijuana. Moreover, the state pointed to a decrease in spending on law enforcement for enforcement of the law. Other states also decriminalized marijuana.

At this point, twenty-nine states and the District of Columbia have passed laws to legalize the use of marijuana for medical or adult recreational use. They have been passed either by referendum (voting) or legislative action. The laws in each state are different, but they allow their residents to ingest marijuana in some fashion without facing criminal charges. Most state laws require a medical diagnosis of specific conditions and a recommendation by a physician before patients are able to use the drug. Most states also require that patients be issued a medical marijuana card that identifies them as legal users. In some states, users are permitted to grow their own marijuana, but in other states this is not permitted. If patients are allowed to grow their own plants, the exact number of plants is determined by the state and varies from place to place. The amount of the product a person can carry is also different. The states where laws permit the use of marijuana are listed in boxes 2.11 and 2.12.

TEXTBOX 2.11.   STATES WITH MEDICAL MARIJUANA LAWS

Alaska
Arizona
Arkansas
California
Colorado
Connecticut
Delaware
Florida
Hawaii
Illinois
Maine
Maryland
Massachusetts
Michigan
Minnesota
Montana
Nevada
New Hampshire
New Jersey
New Mexico
New York
North Dakota
Ohio
Oregon
Pennsylvania
Rhode Island
Vermont
Washington
West Virginia
*District of Columbia

Source: State Marijuana Laws in 2017 Map. Governing the States and Localities. www.governing.com/gov-data/state-marijuana-laws-map-medical-recreational.html

**TEXTBOX 2.12.   STATES WITH
RECREATIONAL (ADULT USE) MARIJUANA**

Alaska
California
Colorado
Maine
Massachusetts
Nevada
Oregon
Washington

Source: State Marijuana Laws in 2017 Map. Governing the States
and Localities. www.governing.com/gov-data/state-marijuana-laws-
map-medical-recreational.html

Many states currently are struggling with how to determine if a driver
is operating a vehicle while under the influence of marijuana (DUIM). It
is not easy to test if a person has been using marijuana and is impaired
in some way. It is accepted that laws should place limits on allowing
marijuana users to drive. Although it is fairly simple to test a driver who
is suspected of being under the influence of alcohol, it is much more difficult to test for marijuana use.

There are currently two ways to determine if a driver is under the influence of marijuana. One is the "per se" Blood Cannabis Content (BCC),
which is used in Colorado and Washington, among other states. The states
that use this test prohibit a person from driving a car if his or her blood
test shows a BCC of 5 nanograms of THC per milliliter of blood. In other
states, particularly Ohio and Nevada, the BCC limit is 2 nanograms per
milliliter of blood. The second test is the "zero tolerance" test. According
to this policy, drivers cannot have any trace of THC in their bloodstream.
If they do, they can be charged with a criminal offense of driving while
intoxicated (or something similar). This would be determined by a blood
test.

The effects of marijuana legalization on driving are a concern to many. It is known that marijuana impairs judgment, reaction times, and motor coordination.[71] However, one study shows that a year after medical marijuana laws were passed in fourteen states and the District of Columbia, there was an 8 to 11 percent decrease in in traffic fatalities. The authors suggest a correlation between legalized medical marijuana and lower consumption of alcohol. Users turn to marijuana instead of alcohol. The authors suggest that alcohol consumption is linked to an increased risk of accidents, which does not imply that a person who drives after using marijuana is safer than one who drives after drinking alcohol. Instead, alcohol is often used in public places such as restaurants and bars, whereas laws prohibit the use of marijuana in public.[72]

INTERNATIONAL LAWS, TREATIES, AND AGREEMENTS

In addition to federal and state laws, there are international treaties and agreements that regulate the sale and trade of marijuana. The Single Convention on Narcotic Drugs passed in 1961 established the International Narcotics Control Board. Seventy-three countries signed on, including countries such as Afghanistan and Mexico, where a significant amount of drugs are manufactured. Over the years, more countries have opted to participate in the treaty. Currently, about 184 countries have signed on. When countries agree to participate, they agree to make the manufacture, trafficking, and possession of marijuana a criminal offense. If a country that has agreed to participate in the convention later decides to legalize the production and possession of recreational marijuana, it is in violation of the convention and it may have a statement condemning its actions made against it, but for the most part there are no serious repercussions. The International Narcotics Control Board was created to implement the convention.

In 1988, the United Nations passed the Convention against Illicit Traffic in Narcotic Drugs and Psychotropic Substances, which is sometimes referred to as the Vienna Convention. If a country agrees to participate in this agreement, it must enact a law prohibiting the possession of marijuana for nonmedical reasons. Those who are convicted of doing so could be sentenced for criminal behavior.

Marijuana has been made legal or decriminalized in other countries around the world in addition to the United States. Officials in Uruguay and the Netherlands decided to legalize it, and Australia and New Zealand are considering new laws that would make medical marijuana legal for their residents.[73] Medical marijuana is currently legal in Israel and in Canada.[74]

CONCLUSION

There is a long history of marijuana use in the United States, both for medical reasons and for recreation. Federal laws ban the manufacture, possession, use, and distribution of marijuana, but many states have passed laws allowing for both. The laws are changing rapidly and will continue to do so. It is difficult to know what the future holds for marijuana, but there is no doubt that debate and changes will continue for years to come.

Chapter Three

The People and
the Politics of Marijuana

Marijuana policies have become political in the United States in recent years, both because of increased public visibility in media as well as increasing acceptance of marijuana use for both medical and recreational use. Many political figures, both elected and appointed, want to see changes in the country's policies; others prefer that no changes be made and that policies remain as they are. As a result, a variety of politicians have made statements or influenced marijuana laws and policies. This chapter provides an analysis of the political aspects of marijuana policy.

THE PEOPLE AND MARIJUANA

The public has become much more accepting of marijuana use and legalization, as shown in chapter 1. That shift in public opinion has resulted (or is linked to) an increased use of marijuana and in how marijuana is depicted in popular culture.

Increased Use of Marijuana

Given that support for marijuana has increased, it is not surprising that more people are using it.[1] Marijuana has become the most frequently used illegal substance around the world.[2] Estimates suggest that about half of all Americans (49 percent) have used marijuana. Further, about 12 percent report that they have used it within the past year.[3] In 2013, about 7.5 percent of Americans aged twelve or older (about 19.8 million people), have used marijuana, an increase from 14.5 million (or 5.8 percent) from

2007.[4] The 2013 "Youth Risk Behavior Surveillance" survey, published by the Centers for Disease Control and Prevention, surveys students in twelfth grade in both public and private schools across the United States. The results of their studies show that 40.7 percent of students in ninth through twelfth grades have used marijuana at least once during their lifetimes. About 8.6 percent reported that they first used marijuana before age thirteen.[5]

Another survey of secondary school-aged students indicates that marijuana has once again become a popularly used drug. Most statistics showed that marijuana use was declining for many years. Results from the "Monitoring the Future Study" in 1992 show that 40 percent of students were using marijuana. Moreover, the percentage of students who perceived a risk related to using marijuana declined from 80 percent to 45 percent from 1990 to 2012. The report indicates that one in fifteen teenaged students admitted to using marijuana either on a daily basis or near-daily basis.[6]

The 2011 "National Survey on Drug Use and Health" further supports this increase in marijuana use. This survey found that the number of people who self-reported that they used marijuana in the past month stayed about the same from 2002 to 2007, but from 2007 to 2010, that number rose by approximately 20 percent. Additionally, the number of respondents who admitted to using marijuana almost every day increased by 38 percent between the years 2007 and 2010.[7]

Not surprisingly, marijuana use in those states where marijuana is legal is higher than in states where it remains illegal. According to the 2013 "National Survey on Drug Use and Health" (carried out by the U.S. Substance Abuse and Mental Health Services Administration), the number of people, ages eighteen and older, in Colorado reporting marijuana use in the previous month is higher than in other states. The figures are listed in table 3.1.

Marijuana Use in Popular Culture

Because of its wider acceptance, marijuana use is often portrayed in popular culture. Its use is seen on television and in movies and heard in music. On television, marijuana use has been openly shown in programs like *Weeds*, *High Maintenance*, *That 70s Show*, *Mary + Jane*, *Weed Country*,

Table 3.1. Marijuana Use during a Three-Month Period, Colorado v. United States

	Total U.S.	Colorado
Ages 12 and Older	12.7	7.4
Ages 12–17	11.16	7.15
Ages 18–25	18.91	29.05
Ages 26 and Older	5.45	10.13

Pot Cops, and *Weediquette*. Marijuana use has also been the topic of shows such as *The Simpsons*, *Family Guy*, *American Dad*, *The Cleveland Show*, *Glee*, and *Parks and Recreation*.[8] Marijuana use can be seen in movies such as Cheech and Chong's *Up in Smoke* and *Still Smokin'*. It is also portrayed in *The Breakfast Club* (1985), *Dazed and Confused* (1993), *Half Baked* (1998), *The Big Lebowski* (1999), *Kid Cannabis* (2014), and *Grow House* (2017). When marijuana is used on these shows and movies, it is typically depicted as comical. At the same time, the dangers of its use are largely ignored. There is rarely a reference to medical marijuana.

Marijuana is commonly referenced in popular music. In the 1930s, Cab Calloway sang about "The Reefer Man" and Fats Waller sang "The Reefer Song." More recently, Ringo Starr sang about giving up marijuana in "The No No Song" in 1975. Not long after, in 1982, the song "Pass the Kouchie" tells listeners to pass the "kouchie" on the left-hand side. Three Six Mafia asks, "Where's Da Bud?" and in Bob Dylan's "Rainy Day Women," he sings that "everybody must get stoned." Afroman explains what he did not do in "Because I Got High." Many others who sing about marijuana use include the Grateful Dead, Snoop Dogg, Dr. Dre, and Cypress Hill. Country music star Willie Nelson not only sings about marijuana, but he also works with NORML on marijuana policy and created his own strain of marijuana.

In addition to drug portrayal in movies and music, many celebrities openly use marijuana or report that they have used it. One is financier George Soros, as is Richard Branson, a billionaire, and Hugh Hefner. Many politicians have used marijuana, including Michael Bloomberg, the former mayor of New York. Former presidents Bill Clinton (who admitted to using marijuana but not inhaling), H. W. Bush, and Barack Obama have all admitted to marijuana use in years past. In 2017 presidential candidate Jeb Bush admitted that he used it—and quickly apologized to his mother. Senator Lincoln Chafee and Governor John Hickenlooper have admitted using marijuana when they were younger. Many actors openly use marijuana. These include Woody Harrelson, Morgan Freeman, Sarah Silverman, Seth Rogan, and Arnold Schwarzenegger. Even successful athletes have admitted to using marijuana illegally. These include Olympic swimmer Michael Phelps and football star Phil Jackson. The late poet Maya Angelou even admitted to using marijuana regularly. Each of these individuals has become extremely successful and wealthy in their fields despite using marijuana.[9] More celebrities who use and support marijuana use publicly are listed in box 3.1.

TEXTBOX 3.1.   CELEBRITIES KNOWN TO USE AND SUPPORT MARIJUANA

Snoop Dogg
Willie Nelson
Wiz Khalifa
Woody Harrelson
Bill Maher
Whoopi Goldberg
Jesse Ventura
Jack Black
Melissa Etheridge
Jack Nicholson
Miley Cyrus

Source: www.nydailynews.com/entertainment/gossip/420-day-stars-support-legalization-marijuana-gallery-1.1064506?pmSlide=1.1064503.

Marijuana Use in the Workplace

The legalization of marijuana, either for medical reasons for recreation, raises many questions about the use of the drug by employees. Should employees be permitted to use medical marijuana on the job? Should employees be permitted to use marijuana recreationally when they are not at work? Since marijuana remains in the bloodstream for weeks, can employees be drug tested and punished for failing a drug test? Are drug tests even relevant anymore?

Moreover, how does marijuana legalization affect the pool of potential employees? Will there be enough potential employees to fill the needs of employers who seek workers who are drug free? Some studies show that youth who use marijuana occasionally over a two-year period are six times more likely to drop out of high school than those who do not. They are also less likely to attend or graduate from college.

Many medical marijuana patients have argued that they should be permitted to use marijuana prior to work or even during work hours. They argue that the marijuana used for medical reasons often does not have the same level of THC that is found in recreational marijuana, and thus they do not experience the same feeling of being "high." Moreover, it is used to treat medical conditions, just like any other prescription drug that may have side effects.

Others who use marijuana for recreational reasons argue that they can use it one day and be "sober" the next, like a person who uses alcohol. The difference between the two drugs is that marijuana remains in a person's system for days or weeks, whereas alcohol is eliminated much more quickly. An employee who uses marijuana days before a drug test may still test positive for THC even though he or she is not under its influence. This is all the more critical because some employers have the right to fire any employee who tests positive on a drug test, regardless of whether he or she is "under the influence" at the time. Readers should be reminded that under federal law the use of marijuana for any reason is illegal.

PUBLIC OPINION AND POLITICAL ACTION

The dramatic changes in public opinion related to marijuana use have resulted in changes to laws in many states. This relationship between public opinion and law is based on democratic theory, in which the laws of a country are based on the popular will of the people.

Democratic Theory

In a democratic system of government, the laws should respond to and reflect the preferences of the citizens who live within it.[10] In general, the preferences of the citizens should have some influence on the policies that are passed by government officials.[11] The laws should be designed in such a way that the interests and concerns of the majority of the citizens correlate to the laws governing them.[12]

If the link between public opinion and policy truly exists and laws are passed that reflect the public's preferences, so, too, should changes in policies when the public's opinions about issues change.[13] Many studies have determined that there is some relationship between public opinion and policies passed by the government[14] but that link may be more or less apparent depending on the specific policy area. One study found a relationship between opinion and policy on only three issues: capital punishment, child labor, and female representation on criminal juries.[15]

The link between public opinion and policy may also change over time. A study of the extent of how policies have changed in light of changes in public opinion found that consistency between public opinion and policy dropped during the course of the study. Policymakers were less responsive to the public's opinions over time, though some topics were more consistent than others.[16]

A more recent analysis of the link between public opinion and policy discovered that a change in public opinion resulted in a change in policy in the majority of situations.[17] Burstein found that the public's opinions on issues result in a policy change about three-quarters of the time and concludes that public opinion has a substantial policy effect,[18] and Agnone shows that public opinion influenced changes in public policy on the environment.[19]

It has been proposed that issues pertaining to "morality" are more likely to reflect public opinion because they reflect the public's notions of what is right and wrong. They also are often policies that can be easily altered by legislators.[20] To that point, one analysis on the relationship between public opinion and gay rights legislation found that there was a significant link between opinion and policy adoption by states.[21] Further, Wetstein and Albritton found that public opinion on policies regarding abortion were less restrictive in places where there is greater public support for abortion.[22]

Of course, public opinion doesn't always dictate policy. The reverse can also occur: legislative changes can impact the public's opinions on that topic. As such, a change in a law may affect the way people think about the problem. This may happen as people learn more about a specific topic and respond by changing their thoughts about it.[23]

Public opinion polls show clearly that more Americans favor legalization of marijuana than in the past. If that is the case, according to democratic theory, marijuana should be legal. However, many popular behaviors are not legal; for example, prostitution, riding motorcycles without helmets, and speeding. We regulate many behaviors for the good of society. Many laws impose limits on personal freedoms, but they also ensure the safety of the individual or others. Although many Americans may support legal marijuana, public health concerns may override those opinions.

An argument made in favor of marijuana legalization is that laws banning use of the plant impose on individual freedoms and liberties. Supporters argue that the drug laws encroach on the private lives of Americans. In essence, all laws infringe on personal freedoms since they restrict behavior in some way. If this argument is applied to all laws, every law would be rescinded. Laws exist to protect not only the individual, but also society as a whole. Laws restricting marijuana use may be doing just that—protecting the individual from long- and short-term physical effects of the plant while at the same time protecting others from reckless behaviors offenders may commit under the influence of the plant.

POLITICS OF MARIJUANA

Politically speaking, those who are elected to office should pay particular attention to the wishes of the public and their constituency (the voters). Elected legislators who pay attention to the concerns of their supporters may be able to maintain or even increase their political support, including their potential reelection success.[24] Conversely, elected policymakers who ignore the public's wishes may fail in their bids for reelection.[25]

Since public opinion has become more accepting of marijuana, more politicians have also become more supportive of marijuana legalization. It is unknown if they are truly in support of marijuana of if they are supporting policies as representatives of their constituents. They may support marijuana legalization only because it is a way to get the public's support and thus their vote.

Nonetheless, political speeches on marijuana have become more common. For many years, politicians supported laws to criminalize marijuana possession and use. In recent years, this has changed. Many politicians are more accepting of marijuana use. The following section documents the changes in political action regarding marijuana.

Presidential Action on Marijuana

Richard Nixon (1969–1974)

President Nixon was the first president to wage war on marijuana. Nixon, a Republican, was strongly opposed to marijuana use and took action against it. He allocated federal money to provide training and equipment to law enforcement, enabling them to more effectively fight marijuana use and distribution. Nixon also implemented Operation Intercept, an attempt to stop the smuggling of marijuana from Mexico. After about three weeks, the program was halted. Very few drugs had been discovered.

Nixon proposed many new policies designed to stop marijuana use in the United States. In speeches, Nixon made it clear that he did not support the use of marijuana. For example, on March 14, 1973, in his annual State of the Union message, Nixon stated:

> I want to emphasize my continued opposition to legalizing the possession, sale or use of marijuana. There is no question about whether marijuana is dangerous, the only question is how dangerous. While the matter is still in dispute, the only responsible governmental approach is to prevent marijuana from being legalized. I intend, as I have said before, to do just that.[26]

Nixon reiterated his dislike of marijuana use in a news conference on March 15, 1973, when he stated very bluntly, "I oppose . . . the legalization of marijuana." This statement leaves little doubt about Nixon's feelings about marijuana use.

As a way to deter people from using marijuana, Nixon proposed new tough antidrug policies.[27] He described these new plans in a radio address about drug abuse prevention, saying:

> In recent days, there have been proposals to legalize the possession and the use of marijuana. I oppose the legalization of the sale, possession, or use of marijuana. The line against the use of dangerous drugs is now drawn on this side of marijuana. If we move the line to the other side and accept the use of this drug, how can we draw the line against other illegal drugs? Or will we slide into an acceptance of their use as well? My administration has carefully weighed this matter. We have examined the statutes. We have taken the lead in making sanctions against the use of marijuana more uniform, more reasonable. Previously, these sanctions were often unrealistic and harsh. Today, thirty-five states have adopted our model statute on drugs, including marijuana. I hope others will. But there must continue to be criminal sanctions against the possession, sale, or use of marijuana.[28]

Nixon then proposed and provided support for the Controlled Substances Act (CSA), which he signed in 1970. Under this law, all drugs were categorized by their medical usefulness and their potential to become addictive. Marijuana was categorized as a Schedule 1 drug, meaning that it had no recognized medical use and a high potential for abuse.

Another provision of the CSA, Section 601, established the National Commission on Marijuana and Drug Abuse. The president was given the responsibility to appoint nine of the commission's thirteen members, including the chairman, Raymond Shafer. Shafer was a fellow Republican and the former governor of Pennsylvania.

After much research, the commission's first report was made public in March 1972. The commission's members indicated that they were skeptical about the apparent link between marijuana use and crime after learning about the drug. In fact, the commission noted that the average marijuana user is not socially isolated nor a severely disturbed individual. The members expressed concerns about the laws that made marijuana use illegal, making note of the expense of enforcing such laws. They stated that the cost of enforcing laws against marijuana outweighed any deterrent effect they might have. However, the members did not go so far as to support new laws to legalize the recreational use of marijuana.[29] Nixon was displeased with the report and largely ignored the commission's findings,[30] instead moving forward with his anti-marijuana policies and declaring a War on Drugs. In 1973, he established a new agency, the Drug Enforcement Administration (DEA), and gave it the power to implement federal laws banning marijuana use.

Gerald Ford (1974–1977)

President Gerald Ford, also a Republican, was not in office long enough to formulate an extensive policy regarding marijuana. When asked about the possible federal decriminalization of marijuana use, Ford said, "I do not believe we have sufficient evidence at the present time to warrant any recommendation in that regard."[31] Instead, Ford focused on providing prevention programs to deter initial drug use, along with treatment programs for those who were addicted to drugs.

Jimmy Carter (1977–1981)

Democratic president Jimmy Carter took little action on marijuana use during his time in office. He considered new policies to decriminalize the use and possession of marijuana but took no action on them.[32] He said, "penalties against the use of a drug should not be more damaging to an individual than the use of a drug itself; and where they are, they should be changed. Nowhere is this clearer than in the laws against the possession of marijuana."[33] Carter halted the practice of spraying marijuana crops with paraquat, a poison that was intended to destroy the plants but was ultimately inhaled by users.[34] Carter also increased funding for initiatives to deter drug trafficking.

Ronald Reagan (1981–1989)

From the start of his administration, Republican president Ronald Reagan supported tough antidrug policies. He thought that marijuana was dangerous for all people, but especially for youth, and should remain illegal.[35] Reagan descried marijuana as a "cunning and treacherous drug" that is "the enemy of our children."[36] Reagan's tough approach to marijuana use included a plan to increase the number of arrests and convictions for marijuana offenses and to seize more of the drug to get it off the streets.[37]

He also solicited the help of the first lady, Nancy Reagan, who told young people to "just say no" if offered drugs (see box 3.2). President Reagan also allowed DEA agents to spray paraquat on marijuana that was being grown in national forest areas, despite the possible health dangers to marijuana users.[38]

Reagan signed the Anti-Drug Abuse Act of 1988 into law. The legislation gave law enforcement the ability to confiscate cash and other property from offeners who profited from their drug activities.

TEXTBOX 3.2. EXCERPTS FROM NANCY REAGAN'S "JUST SAY NO" SPEECH

Today there's a drug and alcohol abuse epidemic in this country, and no one is safe from it—not you, not me, and certainly not our children, because this epidemic has their names written on it. Many of you may be thinking: "Well, drugs don't concern me." But it does concern you. It concerns us all because of the way it tears at our lives and because it's aimed at destroying the brightness and life of the sons and daughters of the United States.

As a parent, I'm especially concerned about what drugs are doing to young mothers and their newborn children. Listen to this news account from a hospital in Florida of a child born to a mother with a cocaine habit: "Nearby, a baby named Paul lies motionless in an incubator, feeding tubes riddling his tiny body. He needs a respirator to breathe and a daily spinal tap to relieve fluid buildup on his brain. Only one month old, he's already suffered two strokes."

Drugs steal away so much. They take and take, until finally every time a drug goes into a child, something else is forced out—like love and hope and trust and confidence. Drugs take away the dream from every child's heart and replace it with a nightmare, and it's time we in America stand up and replace those dreams. Each of us has to put our principles and consciences on the line, whether in social settings or in the workplace, to set forth solid standards and stick to them. There's no moral middle ground. Indifference is not an option. We want you to help us create an outspoken intolerance for drug use. For the sake of our children, I implore each of you to be unyielding and inflexible in your opposition to drugs.

Our job is never easy because drug criminals are ingenious. They work every day to plot a new and better way to steal our children's lives, just as they've done by developing this new drug, crack. For every door that we close, they open a new door to death. They prosper on our unwillingness to act. So, we must be smarter and stronger and tougher than they are. It's up to us to change attitudes and just simply dry up their markets.

So, to my young friends out there: life can be great, but not when you can't see it. So, open your eyes to life: to see it in the vivid colors that God gave us as a precious gift to His children, to enjoy life to the fullest, and to make it count. Say yes to your life. And when it comes to drugs and alcohol, just say no.

Source: Nancy Reagan. "Just Say No" Address to the Nation. September 14, 1986. CNN.com. www.cnn.com/SPECIALS/2004/ reagan/stories/speech.archive/just.say.no.html.

George H. W. Bush (1989–1993)

Like Reagan, Republican president George H. W. Bush fully supported federal policies that banned marijuana. In a 1989 speech from the Oval Office in the White House, Bush promised $7.8 million in federal funds for law enforcement efforts to enforce all federal laws on marijuana,[39] including expanded programs to eradicate domestic marijuana crops.[40]

President Bush often sought the cooperation of international leaders in the fight against marijuana. He cooperated with the leaders of Mexico to help them reduce the cultivation of marijuana by "unprecedented amounts"[41] in the hopes that less would be imported into the United States. In 1990, he signed the U.S. ratification for the United Nations Convention against Illegal Drugs, which was an international effort for all participating nations to "criminalize the production, cultivation, and trafficking in the drugs that are poisoning our kids," including marijuana. The convention supported stronger law enforcement actions to address drug trafficking, including increased efforts to seize the assets of traffickers who purchased goods with profits from their drug activities. The convention also provided support for increased enforcement of anti–money laundering laws and increased extradition of drug traffickers.[42] President Bush supported a zero-tolerance policy when it came to drug use.

Bill Clinton (1993–2001)

As a Democrat, President Clinton was expected to take a different approach to illicit drugs than the previous Republican presidents, but Clinton held many similar views of marijuana as President Bush. Like Bush, Clinton felt that laws legalizing marijuana use would send a message to youth that the drug is safe to use—or that it is even beneficial to health.[43]

President Clinton was not in favor of medical marijuana use, either, explaining that there was no scientific proof to show any clear medical benefits of it. Even after voters in California and Arizona passed initiatives to permit medical marijuana use by its residents, Clinton continued to show his opposition. He made it clear that marijuana was illegal under federal law and that the federal government would not recognize state laws allowing marijuana use. Further, he stated that the federal government would continue to prosecute those physicians who chose to recommend marijuana as a medical treatment.[44]

In 1994, Congress, with the help of President Clinton, passed a new crime bill that resulted in a dramatic increase in the number of people arrested for drug-related offenses. It was reported that in 1991, there were 327,000 arrests for marijuana offenses; in 2000, that number exceeded 700,000.[45] In reaction to this, Clinton allocated funds to provide treatment to those who were addicted to illicit drugs.[46]

George W. Bush (2001–2009)

As a candidate for the presidency, Republican George W. Bush indicated that he would respect the new state laws on marijuana use. However, when he became president, federal prosecutors enforced the federal laws against medical marijuana growers.[47] Bush then continued to support federal laws banning marijuana throughout his two terms in office. In October 2001, DEA agents raided the Los Angeles Marijuana Resource

Center, a marijuana dispensary that provided medical marijuana to patients with serious, chronic health conditions. The agents destroyed four hundred marijuana plants, confiscated equipment used for weighing and packaging the marijuana, and removed information, including the names and medical history of clients. The DEA then raided another dispensary in September 2002, this time entering the WoMen's Alliance for Medical Marijuana, taking the owners into custody, and charging them with intent to distribute marijuana. During this raid, agents seized more than one hundred marijuana plants. The DEA raided a third dispensary in September 2002, and in February 2003, they raided marijuana businesses in ten states as part of Operation Pipe Dream.[48] After this, it became clear that President Bush opposed marijuana use and sought to enforce federal laws, largely ignoring the state laws.

Barack Obama (2009–2017)

Democratic president Barack Obama described his feelings about marijuana at a fundraising event in 2011. He said,

> When it comes to medical marijuana, I have more of a practical view than anything else. My attitude is that if it's an issue of doctors prescribing medical marijuana as a treatment for glaucoma or as a cancer treatment, I think that should be appropriate because there really is no difference between that and a doctor prescribing morphine or anything else. I think there are legitimate concerns in not wanting to allow people to grow their own or to start setting up mom-and-pop shops because at that point it becomes fairly difficult to regulate. I'm not familiar with all the details of the initiative that was passed [in Oregon] and what safeguards there were in place, but I think the basic concept that using medical marijuana in the same way, with the same controls as other drugs prescribed by doctors, I think that's entirely appropriate. I would not punish doctors if it's prescribed in a way that is appropriate. That may require some changes in federal law. I will tell you that . . . the likelihood of that being real high on my list is not likely. What I'm not going to be doing is using Justice Department resources to try to circumvent state laws on this issue simply because I want folks to be investigating violent crimes and potential terrorism. We've got a lot of things for our law enforcement officers to deal with.[49]

Obama seemed to respect state laws that permitted marijuana use. He did not rely on the DEA to raid dispensaries, but instead supported "ignoring" violations as long as marijuana-related businesses abided by state laws. If anything, Obama enforced federal laws against large-scale marijuana distributors as opposed to small, privately owned dispensaries that were regulated by the states.[50]

During the Obama administration, the federal laws prohibiting marijuana were not enforced as long as they did not conflict with federal policy goals and priorities. The federal objectives required that states include provisions in their laws to prohibit marijuana sales to juveniles, tactics to deter participation by criminal organizations in marijuana enterprises, methods to reduce violence, and ways to identify drivers who are driving while under the influence of the drug.[51]

Donald Trump (2017–)

During his presidential campaign, Republican Donald Trump declared his support of medical marijuana but did not mention his views on recreational use of the drug. Once president, Trump and his attorney general, Jeff Sessions, indicated their support of the 1970 Controlled Substances Act. Their position was outlined in a memo written by Sessions that was distributed to federal prosecutors. Sessions recommended that federal prosecutors charge those who violate federal drug laws with the crimes that have the most severe penalties connected to them (see chapter 2).[52]

COURT DECISIONS

Federal courts have reviewed the status of marijuana laws. A California state court has upheld the Rohrabacher-Farr bill. In *United States v. Marin Alliance for Medical Marijuana (Northern District of California)*, 372 F.3d 1047 (2004), the justices ruled that law enforcement cannot shut down dispensary owners who abide by state laws. Because of this decision, the Department of Justice was forced to drop federal charges against a dispensary owner in Oakland in 2011 after it was raided.

In another California case, *United States v. McIntosh*, Ninth Circuit, 124 F.3d 1330 (1997), the justices declared that the Rohrabacher-Farr bill prevented federal prosecutors from charging dispensary owners whose actions were legal according to the laws passed in the state. In order to charge an offender, the prosecutor must show that the defendant violated the state law.

The U.S. Supreme Court also has ruled on marijuana policies. In June 2005, the Supreme Court decided the case of *Gonzales v. Raich*, previously *Ashcroft v. Raich*, 545 U.S. 1 (2005). Here, the justices declared that federal officials could charge medical marijuana patients who used marijuana after being advised to do so by a licensed physician. In doing so, the court confirmed that federal laws on marijuana were valid and that state laws allowing for marijuana use do not preclude users from facing federal charges.

In 2016, the Supreme Court refused to hear a case initiated by officials from the states of Nebraska and Oklahoma to rule on the legality of Colorado's marijuana law, which allows for adult recreational use of the drug. The suit claimed that "the state of Colorado authorizes, oversees, protects and profits from a sprawling $100-million-per-month marijuana growing, processing and retailing organization that exported thousands of pounds of marijuana to some thirty-six states in 2014." Further, "if this entity was based south of our border, the federal government would prosecute it as a drug cartel." Officials from Nebraska and Oklahoma claimed that the Colorado laws that permitted marijuana use violated the federal Controlled Substances Act and therefore should be deemed unconstitutional.[53]

CONCLUSION

Politics plays a critical role in the public's perception of the potential dangers of marijuana. All three branches of government have been involved in the debate over legalization. In theory, the members of these branches act in accordance with the will of the people. In other words, the laws and policies that govern people's behavior should reflect the desires of the majority. There is little doubt that marijuana will continue to be a controversial issue in the near future and that the politics of marijuana will be a large part of the government's agenda.

Chapter Four

The Myths and Realities of Marijuana

Both proponents and opponents of marijuana use (for recreation or for medical reasons) have made many arguments to support their perspectives on the legalization of marijuana. The arguments made on both sides of the legalization issue are often contradictory and can become confusing. This chapter looks at some of those arguments in closer detail.

PROPOSITION 1: MARIJUANA
IS NATURAL AND THEREFORE SAFE

Proponents

For many years, marijuana proponents have argued that marijuana is a natural substance and therefore does not pose health problems for users.[1] Some research supports this and shows that marijuana seems to be a relatively safe substance for human consumption. For example, a UCLA research project indicated that there was some evidence showing that marijuana use may result in some kind of protective effect against cancer.[2] More evidence that marijuana is not harmful was provided by researchers at the University of California at San Francisco, who published their results in the *Journal of the American Medical Association*. These researchers analyzed the medical records of more than five thousand users who smoked marijuana for more than twenty years. They discovered that the majority of people who used marijuana "moderately" did not experience any negative consequences to their pulmonary functions.[3] Another study by the National Academies of Sciences, Engineering, and Medicine concluded that based on their evidence, smoking marijuana does not lead to an increased risk for lung, head, or neck cancer in adults.[4]

A 2015 longitudinal study of marijuana users also found that there were no long-term effects of marijuana use. The researchers interviewed people who had used marijuana at a young age, those who began later in their lives, and those who had never used it. Ten years after they had last used marijuana, the participants were questioned about their health. The findings indicated that there were no differences in physical or mental health among any of the groups. The researchers concluded that excessive marijuana use for long periods of time was not associated with any physical or mental health concerns later in life.[5] However, concerns have been raised about the quality of this study, including the small sample size, the lack of sample representativeness, and missing data.[6]

Opponents

On the other hand, there is evidence showing that marijuana is harmful, and despite being natural, is not safe in the long term. There are many naturally existing substances that are not safe for humans to ingest, including nightshade and monkshood, which are both poisonous. Tobacco is a plant that can cause cancer and other ailments if used over time.

The results of medical studies support the contention that marijuana is harmful to users, particularly to those who use the drug at a young age or who use large amounts of the drug. Some of the studies have shown that marijuana use can lead to lung cancer. One 2013 study found that the risk of lung cancer in those who smoked marijuana over their lifetime increased later in life. The participants admitted to using marijuana when they were between the ages of eighteen and twenty. The findings indicated that those who described their marijuana use as "heavy" during that time had more than a twofold risk of developing lung cancer forty years later.[7] Other studies with similar findings explain that marijuana smoke contains chemicals and tar (carcinogens) that are similar to those found in tobacco. When these are inhaled, they may irritate a user's throat and lungs. Since a person inhales marijuana deeper and holds the smoke in the lungs longer, the impact may be even worse than tobacco.[8]

The World Health Organization (WHO) reported that marijuana smoke is twice as carcinogenic as tobacco smoke. They concluded that marijuana smoke causes carcinoma of a user's lungs, larynx, mouth, and esophagus and can result in other chronic pulmonary diseases. It is common for carcinomas resulting from marijuana use to develop earlier in users when compared to cancers that are caused by tobacco smoke, according to the WHO. The WHO has also concluded that marijuana increases the risk of death in those who have existing heart disease. This is exacerbated because cannabis is now ten times purer than it was in the past, indicating that there can be potentially greater health risks to users.[9]

The results of other studies indicate that long-term use, especially by young users, may result in permanent changes in the brain, leading to decreased cognitive abilities or other adverse changes.[10] Similar research shows that teens who regularly use marijuana report that they often experience problems related to memory, learning, and impulse control. One study that examined the attention span and memory of users and nonusers found that those who used marijuana over a longer period showed impairments in memory and attention spans. Additionally, those memory impairments remained after the person stopped using marijuana. For some people, the issues worsened over the years if it was used regularly.[11]

Additional research has found that there may be significant structural differences in the brains of people who use marijuana when compared to those who do not. Of course, the amount of brain impairment varies depending on the age of the user and the amount of drug consumed. Moreover, the effects are worse if marijuana is combined with alcohol or other drugs.[12]

More evidence of the effect of marijuana use on a user's brain comes from experts at Northwestern University, who found brain changes in teenagers who used marijuana each day for three years when compared to teens who did not. Even two years after the participants stopped using marijuana (participants were then in their twenties), the users experienced problems with memory and other brain abnormalities. The results of the study showed that users who began using marijuana at a young age had even more changes in their brain and memory.[13] Recent users (defined in this study as those who used within the past twenty-four hours) reported problems with learning and memory, as well as a shorter attention spans, even days after they stopped using. Marijuana use among teenagers impairs academic achievement and test scores and even their social relationships.[14]

It appears that the THC in marijuana may have harmful effects on the brain's neurons. Studies show that THC kills the brain cells of newborn and adolescent rats.[15] It is becoming clear that there may be a relationship between smoking marijuana that contains high levels of THC and damage to the white matter in the brain.[16]

Based on these findings, it is not surprising that other research shows that, for some users, marijuana use can lead to changes in a person's IQ. Young people who used marijuana regularly during their teenage years can experience a decrease in their IQ score by an average of eight points over a twenty-five-year period.[17] Results of educational achievement tests are slightly lower among users.[18] Researchers reviewed the records of those who started using marijuana as teenagers and who developed an addiction to marijuana before the age of eighteen. Users' IQ scores declined by eighteen points over time. Moreover, their IQ scores did not increase when they halted their marijuana use. Those who began using marijuana as adults did not experience the same decline in IQ scores.[19]

In a similar study, researchers administered IQ tests to adults who used marijuana as teenagers. According to the study results, users lost on average somewhere between six and eight points on their IQ score. The research also shows that those who quit using marijuana in adulthood did not recover those lost IQ points. It should be noted that similar research concluded that the loss of IQ points may be caused by factors other than marijuana use, such as genetics or family environment.[20]

Studies also find that marijuana use can affect the mental health of users. It has been linked to psychosis in some users, as well as earlier onset of schizophrenia.[21] The more people use the drug, the higher the risk of developing these problems.[22] In some people, marijuana use can cause symptoms of schizophrenia and other psychotic disorders. Other users experience depression and anxiety. Users may experience suicidal thoughts after using marijuana.[23] Females who use marijuana regularly are more likely to suffer from anxiety attacks and depression.[24]

One study of marijuana use and mental health showed that those people who used marijuana, both at early and later ages, showed more signs of depression when compared to those who never used marijuana. This held true even when the level of education was held constant.[25] For those who suffer from bipolar disorder, heavy marijuana use has been linked to stronger symptoms when compared to nonusers.[26] It has also been reported that heavy marijuana users are more likely to report thoughts of suicide than those who do not use.[27] Some have linked marijuana use with symptoms of attention deficit hyperactivity disorder (ADHD). It should be noted that some studies have shown that marijuana use does not lead to an increase in mental health problems.[28] The relationship between marijuana use and depression or other mental health problems may be because people who use marijuana heavily tend to have lower brain responses to dopamine, a chemical associated with pleasant feelings. A study of heavy users found that they had weaker responses to a stimulant (methylphenidate) that increases dopamine in the brain, as compared to people who did not use marijuana.[29]

In some cases, marijuana use may affect a person's heart. A study carried out between 2003 and 2013 on 33,343 men and women, users and nonusers, found that marijuana use affects the heart's inner lining up to ninety minutes after it is used. A user's heart rate increases up to three hours after they smoked. Use increases the risk of heart attack by up to 5 percent.[30] Those who use marijuana have a higher risk of developing stress cardiomyopathy, a weakening of the heart muscle. Use can cause tachycardia and reduce blood flow to the brain. Marijuana use is reported to be a risk factor for cardiovascular disease in young adults. Users can experience sudden cardiac death, stroke, transient ischemic attack, and marijuana-induced arteritis.[31] It should be noted that the evidence linking marijuana with heart attacks and stroke is unclear.[32]

Marijuana use has been linked to pulmonary symptoms including chronic bronchitis, daily or intense coughing, and the overproduction of phlegm (which seems to go away if the person stops using).[33] Many users report inflammation of the large airway, irritated bronchial tubes, increased airway resistance, and lung hyperinflation. Moreover, smoking marijuana may increase a user's chances of contracting pneumonia because of THC's immune suppressing effects.[34]

Marijuana use by pregnant women increases the risk of low birth weight[35] or brain problems and behavioral difficulties. Babies born to women who smoked marijuana have a higher pitched cry and are more likely to tremble. Children born to women who used marijuana had an increased chance of being diagnosed with neuroblastoma, a form of cancer.[36] However, other studies indicate that the evidence linking cannabis use during pregnancy with cancer in the child is only minimal.[37]

More recent studies have linked marijuana use by male adolescents and testicular cancer.[38] It is also thought to reduce the sperm concentrations in men.

Summary

It is still not known if marijuana is safe to use. There is evidence to indicate that there are some negative and detrimental effects of marijuana use, especially long-term use, particularly to young users. It is probably less harmful than other drugs, but it may not be harmless, especially for young people or heavy users. Continued research is needed to know if there are harmful effects of marijuana use.

PROPOSITION 2: MARIJUANA HAS MEDICAL BENEFITS

Proponents

Marijuana proponents claim that marijuana is a safe treatment alternative for a variety of medical conditions. Supporters present evidence that marijuana has medical benefits for many patients and can be used to decrease symptoms associated with many ailments including pain, glaucoma, diabetes, cancer, Alzheimer's, ADHD, migraines, HIV/AIDS, multiple sclerosis, post-traumatic stress (PTSD), Alzheimer's disease, nausea, epilepsy, and Crohn's disease, among others.[39]

Some research has, in fact, found medical benefits of marijuana use. Cannabidiol, a compound in marijuana, seems to have antioxidant effects and works as an anti-inflammatory that may be beneficial to those with Crohn's disease or multiple sclerosis. Another study confirmed the positive effect of giving cannabidiol daily to 137 people (their average age was eleven) who had been diagnosed with epilepsy and who suffered from seizures. At the end of the twelve-week study, the number of seizures experienced by the study participants dropped in half.[40] Results of another study on 171 patients showed that 44 percent of patients who were given a drug based on purified cannabidiol had a significant reduction in the number of their seizures.[41] Similar positive findings resulted from a study by a research team at New York University's Langone Medical Center.[42]

Emerging evidence seems to show that marijuana can be an effective treatment for those who suffer from addiction to opioids. The findings are preliminary and yet to be proven. It has also been reported that marijuana may be helpful to those experiencing withdrawal symptoms associated with alcohol abuse, but there is no scientific evidence to support that claim.[43]

Studies suggest that marijuana has a "modest" effect on adults who suffer from nausea and vomiting resulting from chemotherapy, chronic pain, or symptoms of spasticity related to multiple sclerosis.[44]

Opponents

Opponents challenge the claim that marijuana has medical benefits. They point out that there is no scientific or medical proof that marijuana is a useful treatment for disease. A great deal of the evidence that marijuana has medical value is anecdotal. Many users have described how marijuana has helped with different ailments, but many medical professionals report that these effects are overblown.[45] The medical benefits of marijuana have not been extensively researched or proven to be safe and effective for adults or children by the Food and Drug Administration (FDA) or the medical community.[46] The FDA has not conducted randomized, large-scale clinical trials that have found medical benefits for patients. Many of the ailments for which people use marijuana cannot be tested objectively.[47]

Some studies currently are underway to determine if there are medical benefits to marijuana, but research is sometimes hampered by federal legislation, specifically the Controlled Substances Act, which classifies marijuana as a Schedule 1 drug. As a Schedule 1 drug, the government has identified marijuana as having no accepted medical benefits. The law also limits a researcher's access to marijuana, which is needed to do the research. Some scientists have worked to get marijuana reclassified as a Schedule 2 drug so that it would be easier to access marijuana and carry out studies. One of those groups supporting this recommendation was the National Academies of Sciences, Engineering, and Medicine.[48]

Some evidence suggests that there are no medical benefits of using marijuana—in fact, there may be negative effects of use, as described earlier.[49] In one study, funded by the U.S. Department of Veterans Affairs, scientists reviewed previous research on the effects of marijuana on PTSD patients. They found insufficient evidence that marijuana use helped patients suffering from the condition. In fact, they noted that patients with PTSD who have agitated states or problems associated with anger management may be at a higher risk for serious consequences if they experience adverse effects from using marijuana. However, the authors conclude that more research is needed in this area.[50]

Another study by the U.S. Veterans Affairs reviewed previous research on the effects of marijuana use for patients with chronic pain, pain from multiple sclerosis, and cancer. The results indicated that some patients experienced pain relief, on average, a 30 percent improvement. When looking at long-term pain relief, the study found that there was some reduction in pain intensity over a one-year period, but the effect was small and not clinically significant. For patients with multiple sclerosis, the researchers found insufficient evidence to support the use of marijuana for pain. The same was true for those suffering from pain related to cancer. On the whole, the report indicated that there was limited evidence of the potential benefits of marijuana use for chronic pain.[51]

Nonetheless, some patients who suffer from chronic pain turn to marijuana as a treatment. There is not much known about the efficacy, dose, administration methods, or possible side effects of this treatment option.[52] Part of the problems is that the amount of THC in marijuana differs from plant to plant, and it has been increasing in recent years.[53] This makes it difficult to administer a consistent dosage of the drug as a medical treatment.

Because so little is known about the benefits or dangers of using marijuana to treat medical conditions, most recognized professional medical organizations, including the American Medical Association (AMA) and the American Cancer Society, have issued warnings against using marijuana for medical reasons. Its use has also been opposed by the American Society of Addiction Medicine, the American Glaucoma Foundation, the National Multiple Sclerosis Society, the American Academy of Pediatrics, the American Psychiatric Association, and the American Academy of Child and Adolescent Psychiatry.[54]

PROPOSITION 3: LEGALIZATION
WILL LEAD TO INCREASED QUALITY
CONTROL AND A MORE CONSISTENT PRODUCT

Proponents

If marijuana is made legal, proponents argue, there would be more over-sight of the product that is sold. It could be regulated to maintain safety and quality standards for users as well as to provide for more consistent amounts of THC in the plants. Regulation will ensure the product's strength is more reliable and that there will be no additives or chemicals on the plant. Buyers would know the strain they are using and the level of THC in the product they purchase in order to provide the effect they seek. Moreover, increased oversight will help to prevent young people from having access to the drug.

Proponents also argue that marijuana should be regulated in the same way that alcohol is currently regulated. In this market, private companies are permitted to manufacture, produce, distribute, and sell the product, but they are regulated by state and federal governments. Those who manu-facture, produce, or sell alcohol must apply for a special license from the government and follow rules. If they violate those guidelines, they face punishment and possible license revocation. The government regulates who can purchase alcohol, sell it, and use it, and the circumstances under which they may do so. Marijuana could be treated the same way. States or cities would regulate who would be permitted to grow the plant, how much could be grown, and who could process, sell, and buy it. They can also regulate where marijuana could be used.

Opponents

Opponents of legal marijuana point out that there will be a lack of con-sistency and quality in legal marijuana despite controls regulating the manufacturing process. Plants contain different amounts of THC (thus, the potency also differs) regardless of the oversight placed on grow sites. It is virtually impossible to guarantee consistency since marijuana is a natural plant. This becomes a concern if a patient is using marijuana to treat a medical condition and is seeking a particular effect. Establishing a consistent dosage for patients is difficult when the strength of the drug varies.

Moreover, opponents claim that regulation may not result in less accessibility for young people. Even though most states require patients to obtain a recommendation from a physician and to carry an identification card, it has been shown that it is easy for nonpatients to obtain medical marijuana cards. In Colorado, only about 20 percent of marijuana sales are to people with legitimate medical conditions.[55] This means marijuana is easy to obtain even where it is regulated.

PROPOSITION 4: MARIJUANA USERS CANNOT OVERDOSE ON MARIJUANA

Proponents

An overdose occurs if a user ingests too much of a drug and experiences serious reactions, including death. Marijuana proponents argue that there have been no overdoses resulting from use of marijuana. Generally, when people smoke marijuana, they feel the effects immediately and know when to stop using it.

Opponents

Overdoses have occurred after a person ingested too much of an edible marijuana product. Though there have been no deaths as a direct result of marijuana use, many users have experienced serious reactions that could be considered an overdose. Some users experience psychotic reactions such as anxiety, paranoia, and hallucinations after ingesting too much THC.[56] This can often lead to violent behavior. The Centers for Disease Control and Prevention (CDC) reported twenty-six deaths from marijuana between 1999 and 2007, which were categorized as mental and behavioral disorders resulting from the use of marijuana.[57] The FDA found that that there were "at least some deaths" in patients who used marijuana around the time they died. They indicated that in these cases, marijuana was not the primary cause of death.[58]

Reportedly, an eleven-month-old infant died from ingesting marijuana in 2015, the second year that marijuana was legal in Colorado. The autopsy found a high concentration of THC in the child's urine. His heart failed from a condition called myocarditis, inflammation of the heart muscle. This may have been the first pediatric death to occur as a result of marijuana.[59]

Many edible products contain significant amounts of THC, which may be dangerous for users with little experience using marijuana or those who have not used the drug in a while. These users may not understand that it takes much longer to feel the effects of the drug when it is consumed orally rather than smoked. Consequently, some users continue eating when they do not feel the immediate high, leading to a serious negative reaction.[60] Opponents of legal marijuana argue that the number of accidental overdoses will increase if marijuana is legalized and more readily available. They also point out that in states where marijuana is legally sold, there is increased risk of unintentional use by children who can easily overdose on small amounts of THC.[61]

It is also thought that the chances of a user experiencing an overdose from marijuana may increase because many strains of marijuana being sold today contain more THC than marijuana sold in the past. The THC content of marijuana seized by law enforcement has risen since 1970 from an average of 3 percent to around 7 percent or 8 percent, with some reporting levels up to 20 percent. The effects of using this marijuana are much different. The higher THC levels increase the risk of an overdose, particularly by users who are new to the edibles scene.[62]

PROPOSITION 5: MARIJUANA IS NOT ADDICTING

Proponents

Supporters of marijuana legalization report that marijuana is not an addictive substance. They point out that many people use marijuana only occasionally and have no problem stopping. The majority of marijuana users do not experience withdrawal symptoms when they stop using the drug, nor do they crave the drug if they do not use it regularly. Very few users need to continue using the drug in order to stave off withdrawal symptoms. Consequently, it is clear that marijuana is not an addictive drug that results in a biological or psychological dependence. Supporters say that if users stop using marijuana even after a period of heavy use, they will more than likely not experience symptoms of withdrawal.[63]

Opponents

It is safe to say that for some people marijuana is addictive. Those with addictions to marijuana are said to have "marijuana use disorder" (sometimes referred to as "cannabis use disorder") and describe feeling dependent on the drug. Upon halting use, addicts often experience withdrawal symptoms such as anxiety, irritability, depression, mood changes, nightmares, and/or insomnia within a few days. Other symptoms include a lack of appetite, restlessness, cravings, headaches, and other discomfort. The symptoms usually appear about a week after the user stops and last about two weeks.[64] It is estimated that 2.7 million Americans were dependent on marijuana in 2009 and 1.7 million could be considered to be abusing marijuana; 4.4 million met the criteria to be considered to be dependent on it.[65]

According to some reports, those who use marijuana with greater frequency are more likely to develop "problem" marijuana use. Further, people who use marijuana when they are younger are more likely to develop problem marijuana use.[66] Other reports indicate that using marijuana can cause dependence in about 10 percent of occasional users and between 50 to 90 percent of more frequent users.

Some studies have found that certain individuals are more likely to become addicted than others. For example, people who have been diagnosed with ADHD were about three times more likely to report using marijuana. Additionally, they are one and a half times more likely to have symptoms of marijuana abuse disorder.[67] Users with some form of mental illness or who have a genetic predisposition to addiction are more likely to have symptoms of marijuana addiction.[68] Youths who use marijuana regularly become addicted to marijuana about twice as often as adults. Young marijuana users are four to seven times more likely to experience marijuana use disorder when compared with older users.

It is thought that about 9 percent of users will become addicted to marijuana, and approximately 30 percent will experience some symptoms of marijuana use disorder. Some reports estimate that about one in ten users will experience symptoms of marijuana addiction.[69] Young people (those who use before age eighteen) are more likely to become addicted or dependent than older users. The younger a person is when he or she begins using marijuana, the more likely he or she will become addicted.[70] Young people may become addicted more rapidly than adults because their brains develop so rapidly.[71]

The number of marijuana users who sought assistance from specialists has doubled in the past ten years.[72] Agencies and clinics that treat those addicted to marijuana report that more adolescents are seeking treatment for marijuana than for alcohol and all other drugs combined.[73]

PROPOSITION 6: LEGALIZED MARIJUANA WILL DECREASE CRIME RATES AND PRISON OVERCROWDING

Proponents

It has been argued that legalizing marijuana will result in more crime because increased drug use lowers users' inhibitions toward increased violence. It has been proposed that use may increase feelings of paranoia, leading to violence, or that a person suffering withdrawal symptoms may react violently. However, this does not appear to be the case. One study showed that crime rates in states where marijuana was legal actually had lower crime rates than those states that still ban it. Researchers compared crime rates for both property crimes and violent crimes from 2010 to 2014 in states that changed their laws and those that had not. They found that the crime rates were higher in those states where marijuana was illegal. However, the difference was not statistically significant.[74] Another study found similar conclusions: there was no evidence of a connection between legalization of medical marijuana and crime rates.[75] Much of the violence associated with drugs, the black market, and gangs relates to harder drugs, not marijuana.[76] It has been estimated that the legalization of marijuana could save $7 billion in costs related to law enforcement.[77]

In counties near the border of Mexico, researchers found that there was a "significant" decrease in violent crime, including murders, robberies, and aggravated assault after medical marijuana laws were passed. It was argued that since users could purchase marijuana legally, the drug traf-ficking organizations that supply marijuana were less active, leading to a decrease in crime.[78]

In addition to reducing crime, many proponents of legal marijuana contend that laws permitting marijuana use will reduce prison populations and overcrowding that exists in many state prisons. Fewer offenders will be sent to prison for drug offenses, leading to a decrease in prison popula-tions. Some estimate that about 20 to 25 percent of inmates currently in-carcerated are serving time in prison for violating drug laws. The Federal Bureau of Prisons estimates that about half of federal inmates in 2014 had been sentenced for committing drug-related offenses.[79]

Opponents

Some agree that marijuana use results in more crime. This assessment was backed by U.S. drug czar Gil Kerlikowske and a study led by his office. The results showed that 80 percent of males arrested in Sacramento during the study period tested positive for drugs, most often marijuana. In fact, marijuana was detected in more than 50 percent of the males who were arrested. When arrestees were tested in other major cities (New York, Atlanta, Chicago, and Denver), researchers found similar results.[80]

A long-term study confirmed the link between marijuana use and crime. Researchers followed male marijuana users for a fifty-year span, finding that users were seven times more likely to commit violent crimes than nonusers. They explained the findings by pointing to the changes in brain function that result from long-term use, especially in young people.[81]

One study found that a parent who used marijuana in the past year was more likely to have engaged in physical abuse. Moreover, in those areas where there was a greater density of storefront marijuana dispensaries, there was more frequent physical abuse of children. In other words, those who use marijuana engage in physical domestic abuse more often than those who do not use marijuana.[82]

Opponents also agree that legalizing marijuana will not reduce the number of inmates in prison. They point out that a more careful analysis of prison populations makes it clear that only about 8 percent of inmates in prison were sentenced for violating marijuana laws. Very few offenders are arrested, convicted, and sentenced to prison for long periods for violating marijuana laws.[83]

It is reported that the majority of inmates are first-time drug offenders who have been arrested and convicted of drug crimes. However, they were not sentenced to prison for violating the laws banning marijuana use but instead for testing positive for drug use while on probation or parole. Most offenders are prohibited from using illegal narcotic drugs, and many "test dirty" for drug use when arrested for other crimes and return to prison.[84] In essence, they are not in prison for violating laws on possession or distribution, but for violating probation.

When any illegal behavior becomes legal, the number of people punished for that behavior will decrease. But simply legalizing marijuana may not reduce prison overcrowding. Those offenders who are serving sentences resulting from drug-related crimes will not be released from prison once the laws change. They must remain in the facility until their sentences are completed. In order for prison populations to decrease, politicians (i.e., governors or the president) must pardon current inmates.

Even if fewer people are sent to prison for violating existing laws on marijuana, people will be convicted of new crimes and sent to prison. For example, there will be new laws regarding grow operations and dispensing marijuana, and there will be people who violate these laws and will be sent to prison for those offenses. States will simply replace one type of drug offender with another.

PROPOSITION 7: MARIJUANA IS NOT A GATEWAY DRUG

Proponents

For many proponents, marijuana is not a gateway drug that causes a user to turn to harder, or more serious, narcotic drugs. The majority of marijuana users will not use other more harmful drugs. According to the Marijuana Policy Project, 107 million Americans have tried marijuana at some point, but only 37 million have tried cocaine. Most users will use only marijuana and not progress into more serious drugs.

Opponents

Opponents of marijuana legalization say that marijuana is a gateway drug and that many people who use marijuana are likely to abuse other illegal substances.[85] Evidence from the American Council for Drug Education supports this, reporting that young people who smoke marijuana are up to eighty-five times more likely to use cocaine than those who do not.[86] Other studies show that marijuana use likely increases the risk that a person will develop a dependence on a substance other than marijuana.[87]

A public opinion study of marijuana use found that those who smoked marijuana in the past reported that they were more likely to use marijuana again if they could purchase it legally. The authors of the study suggest that this finding means that legalization "could be a gateway for return to marijuana use among those who have not used in the past year."[88] They suggest this could be the result of decreased stigma and the lessened possibility of legal action.[89]

Legalization of marijuana will also lead to an increased number of users, according to some. In fact, people living in states where marijuana has been decriminalized are 16.2 percent more likely to smoke marijuana than those living in states where marijuana is illegal.[90]

PROPOSITION 8: MARIJUANA
LEGALIZATION WILL ELIMINATE THE BLACK MARKET

Proponents

Proponents argue that legalized marijuana will eliminate the black market production, sale, and distribution of marijuana, replacing it with a legal industry. Users will purchase marijuana from legal dispensaries because the drug is regulated and safe to use. They will no longer buy the product on the street.

Opponents

On the other hand, opponents of legalization claim that legalized marijuana will not eliminate the unauthorized or illegal sale of marijuana. A black market will continue to exist in those places where marijuana is made legal. The taxes on legal sales of marijuana increase the prices, which may make it cost prohibitive to many buyers, who will turn to illegal marijuana, which is not taxed and is therefore much cheaper. Moreover, the black market is attractive to young people who do not meet the age requirements to purchase legal marijuana. In states where recreational marijuana is still illegal, buyers will remain loyal to the black market.

In an analysis of marijuana sales in Holland, where marijuana has been quasi-decriminalized, it is estimated that two-thirds of the marijuana sales occur outside the area where it is legal and regulated (i.e., in the coffee shops). It has been suggested that it could be impossible to sell marijuana in a legal, regulated, and taxed manner to undercut the sales made on the illegal black market.[91]

A study by the RAND Corporation shows that only about 16 percent of a drug cartel's income is related to the sale of marijuana. Most of their money is made by trafficking in other illegal drugs including cocaine, methamphetamine, and heroin. In fact, the United Nations estimated that about one-third of marijuana used in the United States is produced inside the United States, which is up from one-sixth. This means that the United States relies on Mexican imports of marijuana less than it did in the past.[92] If the cartels are blocked from selling marijuana, they simply will sell other drugs or engage in other activities such as the sex trade.[93] So legalizing marijuana use would not decimate the cartels nor stop the violence associated with these organizations.

In order to eliminate the black market for marijuana, officials in states that have legalized marijuana should require a portion of the profits from marijuana sales to be spent on preventing marijuana from being accessible to underage youth. Unfortunately, this does not seem to be the case. One study showed that marijuana use was higher and youth's perception of its riskiness was lower in states with legalized medical marijuana.[94]

PROPOSITION 9: TAX REVENUES
WILL INCREASE AFTER MARIJUANA IS LEGALIZED

Proponents

Some argue that the push for legalization by the states is largely due to the profits and taxes that can be made on sales of marijuana. It is clear that there have been dramatic increases in revenue to the states in which legal marijuana sales are taxed, allowing those states to easily balance their budgets. In fact, this already has happened in states where marijuana sales are already legal and taxed, such as Colorado. Financially, the states where marijuana is legal have made a tremendous amount of money from the sales of the drug. Tax revenue from Colorado are listed in table 4.1.

Table 4.1. Colorado's Tax Revenue from Marijuana

Sales Month	Total	Medical	Recreational
October 2016	$3,304,756	$982,998	$2,321,758
November 2016	$2,980,227	$949,280	$2,030,946
December 2016	$3,217,201	$914,206	$2,302,994
January 2017	$3,056,541	$872,813	$2,183,728
February 2017	$3,534,708	$1,111,314	$2,423,393
March 2017	$3,692,930	$1,076,901	$2,616,029

Source: State of Colorado, Department of Revenue. "Marijuana Tax Data." www.colorado.gov/pacific/revenue/colorado-marijuana-tax-data.

This information shows that Colorado's budget revenue has increased due to the sale of marijuana. Similarly, economists in Oregon estimated that the state revenue will be bolstered by about $210 million in taxes through the middle of 2019.[95] Nationally, marijuana has become the largest retail cash crop across the nation in recent years, greater even than corn, soybeans, and hay.[96] A report from the U.S. State Department in 2005 shows that the cultivation of domestic cannabis in the United States totals about ten thousand metric tons each year, which is more than twenty-two million pounds. This is approximately ten times the amount produced throughout the early 1980s.[97] It is also estimated that the national retail value of domestic marijuana sales could be as high as $113 billion annually, which is close to that of alcohol (which is legal and advertised).[98] The sales of marijuana are predicted to increase yearly as indicated in table 4.2. This clearly shows that there will be a massive growth in profits from the sale of marijuana, both recreational and medical, in the future.

Legalized marijuana also provides employment opportunities for thousands of people. This includes not only those directly involved in marijuana sales, such as growers, manufacturers, bakers, and retail sales

Table 4.2. Projected Marijuana Sales

Year	Recreational (billions)	Medical (billions)	Total (billions)
2016	$1.8	$2.2–2.7	$4–4.5
2017	$2.6–2.9	$2.5–3.2	$5.1–6.1
2018	$3.8–5.0	$2.9–3.8	$6.7–8.8
2019	$5.4–7.3	$3.1–4.3	$8.5–11.6
2020	$6.4–8.6	$3.7–5.1	$10.1–13.7
2021	$7.1–10.3	$4.8–6.8	$11.9–17.1

Source: Chris Walsh (2017, May 17). Presentation. Marijuana Business Conference and Expo.

employees, but also those in the secondary market, which includes those involved in the tourism industry, those who sell growing equipment, those who provide security to grow sites, realtors, restaurant owners, lawyers, CPAs, branding and marketing experts, advertising agents, those who manufacture products to transport the plants, distributors, compliance agents, labeling printers and experts, contractors, landlords, equipment sales, security, insurance agents, light, air, heat, water, grow medium, nutrients, planters, harvests, drying, storage, packaging, bookkeeping, office assistants, personnel, trimmers, and many, many others. In early 2017, there were more than 120,000 full-time, legal jobs in marijuana-related businesses.[99] The number of employees in the cannabis industry is estimated to be between 165,000 and 230,000.

Opponents

States with legal marijuana have all struggled with how to tax the sale of the product. If officials set high taxes, it may limit people from purchasing the product (and thereby consumption of it) simply because it raises the cost. On the other hand, if taxes are set too low, the state will lose money. Low taxes also might result in increased use by juveniles and others who should not use it, since the cost will be lower and more affordable.[100]

Although tax revenues will increase in places where marijuana sales are taxed, there will be new costs, as well. New laws will be established related to oversight of growing operations, dispensary operations, or use of the drug, which did not exist before. Law enforcement must enforce the laws and arrest those who violate the laws. Thus, the costs will be transferred to new offenses.

There also may be increased costs associated with health care. Some users will become addicted and need treatment. Others may suffer permanent brain damage or impaired brain development, which will require long-term assistance. Some users may be diagnosed with depression or schizophrenia related to their drug use or even participate in criminal behavior. There will also be an increase in those who drive impaired, become involved in domestic violence, and are unable to find jobs. It will become necessary to provide additional social programs, which cost a lot of money.[101] Although many of the costs associated with marijuana legalization are still unknown, there is no doubt that there will be additional costs that will burden state budgets, which will offset the high tax revenues from the sales of marijuana.

PROPOSITION 10:
MARIJUANA SHOULD BE RESCHEDULED

Proponents

Proponents argue that marijuana should be recategorized as a Schedule 2 drug. As a Schedule 1 drug, marijuana is not recognized as having medical benefits. The drug is strictly regulated and banned from use by patients. As a Schedule 2 drug, it could be tested to determine medical benefits and possible side effects. Proponents argue that rescheduling marijuana would result in a more accurate reflection of the safety of the drug, as well as its pharmaceutical and chemical characteristics.

Some proponents of legalization view the push for rescheduling in a different light and do not want marijuana rescheduled. They point out that the ever-growing marijuana industry exists only because marijuana is a Schedule 1 drug. If it were rescheduled, it would be then be considered a pharmaceutical drug by the federal government and the FDA, resulting in studies to determine its effectiveness as a drug, proper dosing, and possible side effects. Marijuana would no longer be sold in dispensaries and instead would be sold only through pharmacies. It would be under the auspices or authority of the FDA, which would regulate and limit its use and sale.

Opponents

Opponents of marijuana legalization seek to retain marijuana's Schedule 1 designation. They believe that the potential social costs related to marijuana use outweigh any potential benefits. The social costs impact the lives, education, and careers of people who are arrested and sentenced for marijuana-related offenses. Each year, thousands of people are harmed by marijuana. Their personal relationships with family and friends are affected; some even lose their housing and employment.[102]

CONCLUSION

There are many arguments made in support of marijuana legalization, but just as many exist to maintain its current status as an illegal substance. The arguments on both sides can be confusing, which is made worse by evidence that seems to support both sides. More research will help the public understand the possible risks and dangers of recreational and medicinal use of marijuana.

Chapter Five

A Medical Perspective

Members of various professions have different ideas about how the legalization of marijuana will affect them and how they carry out their jobs. When asked questions regarding their opinions of new laws allowing for marijuana use, respondents in various professional groups—medical professionals, law enforcement/security, legal professionals, and educators and students—provided very different comments. All respondents were asked similar questions, including (1) how marijuana legalization affects their jobs; (2) if marijuana is a gateway drug; (3) whether medical marijuana should be legal; (4) whether recreational marijuana should be legal; and (5) what laws permitting marijuana use should include.

MEDICAL PROFESSIONALS

Medical professionals must interact with people who have used marijuana and manage any medical conditions resulting from that use, which can include short-term physical reactions like anxiety attacks or hallucinations or perhaps long-term consequences such as cancer. In states where medical marijuana is legal, medical professionals must decide whether to prescribe marijuana to patients, and if so, to which patients and under what circumstances.

Those participating in this analysis have been members of the medical profession for periods ranging from four months to forty years. These professionals hold a various of positions within the medical field, including EMT, paramedic, nurse, physician assistant, family doctor, optometrist, and psychologist.

How Will Legalized Marijuana Affect Your Job?

Many respondents noted that legal marijuana would not affect their job to any great degree. Some explained that their current calls are not primarily from people who have used marijuana, possibly because it is an illegal behavior. One respondent explained that the low number of marijuana-related calls was because it is difficult to overdose on marijuana.

Some respondents were unsure if more people would use marijuana if it was made legal and how that would affect the number of calls they received for help. Many predicted that more people encountered by medical professionals will be using marijuana, using more marijuana than before, or using marijuana combined with other drugs. They predicted that increased use will probably lead to more instances of misuse of the drug, resulting in more calls to help people who have used too much, mixed marijuana with other drugs, or need help for other marijuana-related reasons. Some users may be "first-timers" who are not familiar with the effects of the drug. There may be additional calls for medical help by those who have ingested too much and are unable to walk or are otherwise sickened by the drug. People may have more accidents resulting from using increased amounts of marijuana. One respondent said, "they may also do stupid things while high and need medical help. I may have to deal with more and more patients who are under the influence of the drug. Some of these patients are hard to handle because they are not thinking straight; some don't respond well to medical treatment." It was suggested that some people will use marijuana because it is easy to obtain rather than other, more dangerous drugs.

The legalization of marijuana may change the treatment options for emergency caregivers. Medical professionals must take into account if a patient has used marijuana, how it was used (smoked or edible), and how much. Since there is no currently accepted way to test for marijuana use, there is no way to know what drug a person has used. Instead, medical professionals must rely on patients reporting what they used. Patients who call for help after using marijuana are sometimes difficult to handle. There are often problems communicating with users and it can be more difficult to treat them. Most people are hesitant to tell doctors or EMTs that they have used drugs, making treating them more challenging.

It is interesting that a small number of medical professionals predicted a decrease in calls for help because patients will be in less pain. Some will no longer need professional assistance to help handle the pain of their medical conditions.

Most medical professionals indicated that even if marijuana is legal, they will not be able to use it. One respondent explained that most people in the medical field are tested regularly for drugs and will lose their jobs if they test positive for marijuana. Marijuana, whether for medical reasons or for recreation, will still be banned for these professionals even if it is made legal.

As one respondent said, the legalization of marijuana will result in happier co-workers.

Is Marijuana a Gateway Drug?

The majority of health professionals interviewed for this study agreed that marijuana is not a gateway drug and does not cause people to use other drugs. They reported that many people use marijuana once and do not want to use other drugs or even use marijuana again. Some admitted that there are drugs that are gateway drugs but marijuana is not one. Respondents explained that most marijuana users have likely used marijuana in the past and consider it is a "safe" drug. They believe that marijuana is natural and for the most part does not result in other health effects akin to tobacco or alcohol use. Most people don't want to take a risk with harder drugs.

On the other hand, some medical professionals stated that marijuana is a gateway drug, explaining that people will use harder drugs and use them more often after trying marijuana because they want to know how other drugs will affect them. If users do not like the effects of marijuana or if they want other effects, they will use other drugs. They may want to use other drugs to experience a stronger high or a different kind of high. In short, these respondents believed that marijuana use causes people to try other substances and to continue to get high. Others explained that marijuana is a gateway drug in the sense that it may make users more comfortable with the lifestyle associated with using illegal drugs or it may expose them to drug dealers and others who sell or use harder drugs.

Some medical professionals did note that marijuana may be a gateway drug for some individuals but that it is not the drug itself that causes more drug use, but rather the individual's personality. They explained that marijuana can be a gateway drug for individuals who are suffering from mental illnesses or those who have addictive personalities. One person noted that it can be psychologically addictive for some people.

Should Medical Marijuana Be Legal?

The majority of medical professionals believe that marijuana should be legal for medical purposes. A typical response was "if it helps people who are suffering from pain related to a chronic illness, they should be able to use it." Another respondent said, "why not let patients use anything that helps them feel better or that may actually treat whatever symptoms they are having?" A long-term professional said, "anything that can help someone medically, I'm all for it. The bottom line is to help patients."

Some respondents noted that marijuana has many medical benefits and can be used to help a variety of medical issues. For example, it was noted that marijuana can be a powerful pain killer; it can be used to treat post-traumatic stress disorder (PTSD), multiple sclerosis (MS), seizures, cerebral palsy, malnutrition, Crohn's disease, irritable bowel syndrome (IBS), anxiety, glaucoma, depression, and cancer. It has been linked to helping people who are undergoing cancer treatments tolerate the side effects of chemotherapy. It helps reduce nausea, enabling patients to eat. In general, "it helps people get through the day and do things they need to do." In short, doctors should be able to prescribe marijuana if patients are diagnosed with these disorders.

Others noted that marijuana can be safer for patients than some pills or other prescribed medicines that are currently used to treat medical ailments. Marijuana does not have the same long- or short-term side effects as many medicines and it is cheaper, explained a few professionals. It can help in cases in which there are no prescription drugs available to treat the condition or in which the prescription drugs either don't work or cause other serious side effects. In most cases, there are no (or only minimal) side effects from marijuana. As one respondent said, "if opiates are legal, marijuana should be, too. It is far less dangerous and is effective for pain management."

One doctor noted that she did not agree with legalizing medical marijuana and stated clearly that she will not prescribe marijuana to patients but admitted that many doctors would. She explained that there is no definite evidence that medical marijuana has any medical benefits. It has never been medically or scientifically proven to treat symptoms; only anecdotal evidence exists. There are no studies that show how marijuana interacts with other drugs. Further, there is no way to regulate dosage, so it is hard to prescribe. It is self-regulating, which is not an effective medical treatment. In the long run, she reported, marijuana could do much more harm than people realize.

Should Recreational Marijuana Be Legal?

Many of the health care professionals agreed that the state or federal government should legalize recreational marijuana. One person argued that, for responsible adults, using marijuana is no different than having a couple of alcoholic drinks, and it calms people down. It may even be safer or healthier. Both alcohol and tobacco, which are legal, have known health effects. Plus, marijuana is not addictive, whereas other legal drugs are. Additionally, if it was legal, marijuana could be regulated and the level of THC in the plant could be maintained as well. The product would be safer if the government regulated it rather than relegating it to the black market.

One of the arguments made in support of recreational marijuana was the money that could be made in taxes. Multiple professionals agreed that marijuana should be taxed and the money given to the schools, used to fix roads, or allocated wherever needed. It would also create jobs, adding to the tax base. One person said, "in Colorado they are making millions off of marijuana, so the money can be really useful." Another professional wrote that marijuana should be legalized for recreational purposes so we can "tax the shit out of it." However, one respondent argued that marijuana should not be legalized, because then it becomes just another drug "for the government to regulate and tax so they can profit. It is just another way to control people."

One professional pointed out that if recreational marijuana is made legal, the crime rate will go down. There will be fewer people fighting over who can sell marijuana in neighborhoods, and there will also be "fewer burglaries and thefts. If it is legal, people will not be arrested for using it or possessing it."

Some of the health care professionals disagreed and argued that marijuana should not be legal for recreational purposes. This was because of its unknown long-term effects, which may result in other medical problems in the future. Some argued that it is too dangerous to legalize. They noted that smoking anything is unhealthy. One person was concerned that people who should not use marijuana (specifically young people) will have access to it. She said, "it is hard to make sure that it is only used by responsible adults and not kids." Others note that marijuana is a drug and therefore can be harmful to users and that the government should not allow people to get high simply because they want to. The respondent explained, "there is no point to smoking marijuana if it is not for a medical reason."

Another reason for maintaining the illegal status of marijuana was provided by one professional who pointed out that if marijuana is legalized, police will be responsible for enforcing the regulations pertaining to regulating all aspects of the plant—from growing to selling and use. There will be costs associated with that. Legalization also reduces the number of police-issued fines that are often related to marijuana. "If we legalize marijuana, police can't issue tickets and get fines. Plus, legalization will make it too easy for kids to get."

It was predicted that recreational marijuana will increase the number of accidents (like DUI or similar offenses) due to an altered state of mind, feelings of invincibility, or the sense of freedom or right to use the drug. It was often noted that "people do stupid things when they are high."

What Are Some Consequences of Use?

One medical professional stated that there are no short- or long-term consequences of legalizing marijuana, whereas another said that we do not know what the long- and short-term consequences are. A third responder described one consequence of legalizing marijuana is abuse: "they will try to use it too much, or someone who is too young (underaged) will use it. Others will try to sell it or take it to another state where it is not legal." Some other predicted consequences include those listed in box 5.1.

One health care professional stated that the worst consequence is that people will expose their children to secondary smoke from marijuana. Another said that some people will make a lot of money, explaining that the legalization of marijuana, both medical and recreational, is all about money. "Those doctors who choose to prescribe it will become known for that and will have many patients come to see them. People who grow it and sell it will make millions. Very little money will really come back to the people. The government will say they will give it to the schools or

TEXTBOX 5.1.   LONG-TERM
CONSEQUENCES OF MARIJUANA USE

- Increased tax dollars to local governments. They would make a lot of money that can be used to improve the communities, schools, or whatever is needed
- Increased violence. There will still be gangs that sell marijuana or want to grow it and people who steal it from others
- Increased use of the drug across all age groups. Young people may use it more for fun; older people for fun and for medical reasons
- Happy citizens
- Reduced crime
- Fewer sick people (because it can help cure illnesses)
- Increased arrests as people grow it illegally
- Increased use and abuse of the drug, maybe even by people who shouldn't use it (i.e., children)
- Job loss by employees who fail drug tests
- Increased accidents—not just car accidents, but all kinds of accidents leading to an increase in emergency calls for medical help
- Job creation
- Healthier, happier people

whatever, but that won't happen as much as it should. Politicians, interest groups, sellers, growers, etcetera will all make a lot of money."

What Should a Marijuana Law Entail?

There were many suggestions from health care professionals about the ideal marijuana law. Many suggested that a law should restrict who can buy it and where they can use it (similar to alcohol). In general, many respondents agreed that the laws should regulate the industry tightly so that kids can't access marijuana. There should be a strict limit on how much people can have and how often they can buy it, that way people aren't likely to give it to someone else or to someone who might be under age or to use it too often or overindulge when they do. Many professionals agreed that marijuana should be taxed and that the money should go to schools and roads. One suggestion was to tax recreational marijuana but not medical marijuana.

It was made clear that the government should oversee growing of the drug. Suggestions included licensing individuals who grow and sell it. Anyone who meets the licensing requirements should be able to sell it, not just those who have a lot of money or who know the right people. One professional suggested that farmers grow and sell to help the U.S. agricultural system.

Suggestions for regulating recreational marijuana included an age restriction (people should be at least eighteen, though some noted twenty-one) to buy it. Other suggestions for medical marijuana included requiring a doctor's prescription along with a mandatory prescription renewal every six months. Medical marijuana should be legal only with a doctor's prescription, and doctors should prescribe it only for chronic illnesses. Doctors should determine what patients could benefit from use, the dosage, and what strain of marijuana to use.

One person noted that it doesn't really matter what the law is. Whether legal or not, people will continue to abuse and smoke marijuana. A law won't affect how many people use it or why they use it. If someone wants to use it, he or she will do so. Many people currently use it for recreational or medical reasons and it isn't legal.

CONCLUSION

Medical professionals share some perspectives on the legalization of marijuana, yet their viewpoints vary greatly in other respects. As a whole, the profession has a wide variety of ideas and predictions about how legalization will affect their jobs—some predicting that there will be no impact, but others predicting more serious effects. Many similar trends can be found throughout the profession, particularly revolving around the possible dangers of marijuana use to young people and the suggestion that marijuana, if made legal, should be taxed for the revenue potential. There are many unknowns about these new laws, and members of the medical profession will need to adapt to the legalization trend and the ensuing changes that will certainly occur in the field.

Chapter Six

A Legal Perspective

LAW ENFORCEMENT/SECURITY PROFESSIONALS

Although there are a variety of perspectives within many fields regarding the legalization of marijuana, those engaged in law enforcement or other legal professions tend to have a unique perspective. This perspective, in some ways, is informed by their experiences. Students, on the other hand, tend to have very different opinions. This chapter analyzes opinions on legalization from respondents in law enforcement, legal professions, and students.

How Will Legalized Marijuana Affect Your Job?

Some officers reported that marijuana legalization will have minimal impact on their jobs since, as one officer explained, lots of people already use it now anyway. Those who want to use marijuana do so even if it is illegal, and most do it safely. Those who wait to use it until it becomes legal won't get crazy. For the most part, the people who use it for medical reasons are not the ones who go out and do weird things. Instead, the people who use opiates and meth are the crazy ones. They use too much and do outrageous things. Another person noted the danger of heroin, blaming it for more harm than marijuana. He said that the heroin epidemic is far worse than marijuana use and causes more problems for the police.

Many law enforcement professionals predicted that marijuana legalization will not affect crime rates or the number of calls they respond to. There may be a crackdown on driving while under the influence of marijuana (as opposed to alcohol). However, this professional noted that "I have always said, and still believe, that alcohol has caused more damage and ruined more lives than marijuana ever will."

Interestingly, one police officer claimed that only about 10 percent of the people he encounters are using some kind of drug, although he encounters the odor of burning marijuana on a regular basis. Because of this, he did not feel that marijuana use was a serious problem for law enforcement.

On the other hand, many officers believed that marijuana legalization will make their jobs more difficult. One officer explained that he sees a lot of people who are using marijuana, as well as a lot of drivers who have pot or other drugs in the car when they are stopped for traffic offenses. He noted that too many drivers are under the influence of some substance. They try to deny that they are using drugs, but the smell is too obvious. He explained that when you open the door and the smell is overpowering, you know that they've been smoking. He noted he is afraid that more drivers will be impaired if marijuana was legal, leading to more accidents, injuries, and deaths. Offenders who are under the influence can be difficult to handle, as well.

One law enforcement professional maintained that marijuana should remain illegal because "it is a dangerous drug and it makes people do crazy things. Users don't think straight. Plus, we don't know what the long-term effects are. It will be crazy when marijuana is legal. And people are growing marijuana in their backyards so there is a virtually unlimited supply."

An officer who is responsible for recruiting new officers expressed a different concern. He explained that the problem with marijuana legalization in law enforcement is mostly with new recruits. Many of the young recruits have used marijuana in the past six months, and they cannot be hired. He said, "Who will we recruit? We do drug testing so they cannot use and expect to keep their jobs as police officers. We would have to talk to legal about anyone who uses marijuana for medical reasons."

The biggest problem for law enforcement, according to one officer, is the lack of a testing procedure to determine if someone has been using marijuana and is able to drive safely. He said the police department currently uses the same initial testing for impaired driving as they do for alcohol use, but if the driver tests negative for being drunk and it seems as if they are under the influence of something, they will bring in an officer with specialized training to identify what drug a person has used, if any, based on behavior and other factors. However, this is subjective and can lead to lawsuits.

One officer with a more negative perspective said that the police will continue to confiscate property of people who use drugs because the police can profit from selling any seized items. Law enforcement will enforce federal marijuana laws because they want the money they get when the property is sold to the public. He said, "If they confiscated all of the stuff [items] from stores in Denver, they can make a lot of money."

Many law enforcement officers indicated that as officers, they can't personally use marijuana for either medical or recreational reasons. They are regularly tested and would be fired if they tested positive for drugs.

Police made many predictions about what might happen if marijuana was legal. One officer predicted that if marijuana is legalized, people—especially juveniles—may use more of it. Even if it is legal only for people eighteen and older, more people under the age of eighteen will use it. Another officer predicted that there will be more crime but a different type of criminal behavior, since crime changes when people are under the influence of drugs. There will be more "stupid" crimes (trespassing) as opposed to violent crimes. More people will do things they wouldn't normally do if they weren't high. Additionally, legalization will make law enforcement more complicated at times because people under the influence of marijuana don't remember events or they don't want to tell on others. Another respondent noted that if marijuana is legalized there will be less paperwork because fewer people will be arrested.

Is Marijuana a Gateway Drug?

Members of the law enforcement profession were unclear as to whether marijuana is a gateway drug. Many were unsure if marijuana use causes future use, but others clearly believed that it does, especially among those with addictive personalities. One officer explained that whether marijuana is a gateway drug depends on the people with whom that user associates. In other words, a person's friends can have a big impact on what they do. If their friends smoke, then they probably will, too. Another professional explained that marijuana is a gateway drug. Users start with pot and then move to harder drugs and become addicted. Once addicted, they will use whatever they can—they don't care what they use to get high. A lot of them start with pot when they are young and then can't stop using.

Another professional indicated his concern that marijuana may be a gateway drug for young users, particularly those in their early teens. He said, "I have seen a few young people who made a habit of 'waking and baking' in their early years, and now they are having a hard time and are using other drugs. Maybe a coincidence, I'm not sure. From my experience, it just seems like young brains shouldn't be exposed to marijuana, alcohol, or any other drugs."

One officer stated very clearly, "I know a lot of people use heroin and probably a lot started on pot. I really don't care if it is a gateway drug. I just know that too many people are dying from heroin and by the time we get to them it is too late."

Should Medical Marijuana Be Legal?

Some law enforcement professionals argue that marijuana should be legal for medical reasons because it has medical benefits. One respondent explained that "it has been used for centuries by people all over the world, so it clearly has some kind of effect for people who are sick; if it didn't it wouldn't be used for so long." The benefits include restoring appetite and reducing the number of seizures patients have. "I am sure there are more benefits," he continued, "but those are two that I'm familiar with."

One professional had firsthand experience: her father used medical marijuana to relieve pain. The officer explained that her father wasn't going to drive anywhere; he didn't go anywhere—he was too sick to leave home. He used marijuana although it was illegal at the time. Marijuana made him more comfortable. He was able to eat and converse more. Because of that experience, the officer supports medical marijuana. Other law enforcement professionals dispute that marijuana should be legal for medical reasons. As one professional put it, "if I were in a lot of pain, I would use the medications prescribed by my doctor. The doctor has lots of 'good stuff' that can be used that doesn't affect your brain, so that is the way to go."

A professional with strong ideas about this subject said, "We don't go to a special store for each drug we take, so why are there special stores for this drug? People are not allowed to make their own aspirin or antibiotic;

why should they be able to grow their own pot? It should be sold at Rite Aid or CVS for a true medical reason, not a stubbed toe or a headache. But first, marijuana has to pass FDA medical tests for specific uses and for specific ailments. We also need to know doses before it can be legal, and right now we don't know that."

Should Recreational Marijuana Be Legal?

Some law enforcement professionals responded to this question by saying that recreational marijuana should be legal for those who are twenty-one and older. They supported proposals to tax marijuana sales to make money. Conversely, some in law enforcement say that marijuana should not be legalized for recreation because it will lead to more crime. One officer said that if marijuana is legal, "more people will use it more. They will commit crimes to get money to buy it." Not only will crime increase, but many pointed out that more people will be arrested for doing stupid things after using marijuana. It will also affect the number of people pulled over for DUI offenses, and it may result in more accidents. In Colorado, there has been an increase in accidents following legalization.

Some believe that making marijuana legal will shut down the black market. "Almost daily our K9 officers are intercepting packages of marijuana at UPS, FedEx, or the USPS. We should make it legit and put the smugglers out of business."

Other professionals pointed to different impacts of marijuana legalization. "Some will commit crimes but mostly they can't find jobs so they sleep in the park or on the street. There will be more people homeless." A potential civil rights issue was brought up by one officer. He predicted that there may be an increase in court cases. He explained that "there is no way to test for marijuana use so police must go by smell. This is troublesome because there may be a driver who is not using, but we must arrest him or her if a passenger is smoking and the car smells of the drug. The driver may be charged when he or she is not using."

Another argument against marijuana legalization was based on moral grounds. One professional said that society must draw a line as to what is acceptable behavior. "Drug use is not good for anyone. People cannot function on drugs, so they should not be legal." Another officer said, "the proliferation of marijuana use can lead to more widespread access to drugs, especially to juveniles. Why encourage any kind of drug use? We have so many problems as it is, we shouldn't tell kids that drug use is OK in any way. [There are] too many heroin ODs."

"Young kids shouldn't be using it, but they will. That's the bad thing. If adults want to, it's their choice, but a young kid shouldn't be using it. No one would agree to that. When kids use it, they are screwed up for the rest of their lives. Parents need to make sure their kids aren't using, but when the parents use, the kids do, too. They see their parents using and think it is safe. Schools try to stop it, but they can't. It's the parent's job."

What Should a Marijuana Law Entail?

Law enforcement professionals offered many suggestions regarding how marijuana laws should be written. They are described in box 6.1.

TEXTBOX 6.1.   LAW ENFORCEMENT'S SUGGESTIONS FOR LAWS FOR LEGALIZED MARIJUANA

- Marijuana should be legal only for those ages twenty-one and older
- Marijuana must be grown in controlled situations and sold at pharmacies
- Marijuana laws must be enforced so young people don't have access to it
- Marijuana should be taxed but not too high or it will cause more crime
- Only medical marijuana should be legal and only when prescribed by physicians
- Laws for legal marijuana should resemble alcohol laws. Users should be twenty-one and older and driving under the influence is not permitted. Public use (smoking) should be restricted.
- Marijuana should tested to determine possible benefits of use
- Tax proceeds from sales of marijuana should go to schools, to programs to provide opportunities for children, and to police.
- Marijuana dispensaries must be monitored to ensure they don't sell to people who shouldn't get it.

LEGAL PROFESSION

The members of the legal profession included in this study were lawyers, prosecutors, magistrates, and court administrators from Ohio, Arizona, and Virginia who ranged in age from new graduates to those who have been practicing for "many" years.

How Will Legalized Marijuana Affect Your Job?

Many professionals in the legal profession reported that marijuana legalization will not affect their job at all. Some attorneys explained that they (or their firms) do not take marijuana-related cases, so there would be no impact for them. According to one judge, his job is to apply the laws to individual cases. He said, "I look at the evidence, hear testimony from people involved in the case, or look at a person's prior record and apply a sentence based on the facts of the case. A large percentage of the cases that I hear are not related to marijuana, so it won't impact me that much."

Another law professional agreed that legalizing marijuana will not affect those in the field too much. An employee in a local county court explained that there may be fewer possession-related cases, but there currently are not many of those types of cases anyway. She said that the county has largely decriminalized possession of small amounts of marijuana so there are not many cases. Large-scale possession cases are either state or even federal cases. She explained further that marijuana legalization may affect lawyers who practice employment law because there will be a lot of cases in which people use medical or recreational (legal) pot and then get fired, especially when legislators are beginning to write the law. But for most lawyers, marijuana legalization will not affect them to a great degree.

Many respondents implied that the legal professional will not change because legal marijuana does not lead to more crime. "Marijuana use does not cause a person to commit crime. There is no statistical evidence that I have seen that shows that people who use marijuana commit crime. Some do, but not everyone. Legalizing marijuana may reduce crime by lowering the number of incarcerated youth, especially from minority communities. Besides, most marijuana users are 'calm, dude.' They don't have the energy to commit crime. It has not led to more crime where I live."

Other attorneys noted that the types of cases may change. Though there may be fewer people arrested for some crimes, there will be more people arrested for other crimes. "It will be a wash. It really won't have an impact on the courts because the number of cases will remain the same." One attorney stated, "Legalizing it won't affect my job. There are so many criminals anyway, it won't make any difference to me." Another agreed. He explained that if the state gets rid of all the minor marijuana cases, it wouldn't affect his office too much. "We still have thousands of other cases to handle. The few people who are in the system for a minor misdemeanor of marijuana use or possession don't matter. It's the ones who have lots of offenses—and they will probably be back again and again."

Another professional agreed that legalized marijuana would not affect his job directly, but he noted that he may have more cases. He explained that though there may be fewer arrests for possession charges, "some people will do dumb things so they will keep getting arrested. I will have clients who use and I'll have to represent them." "A lot of users can't keep a job so they have to use a public defender, but they'll be back in the system before too long. They'll just keep using drugs and committing crimes. Doesn't matter what the laws are."

If laws permitting recreational marijuana are passed, according to one lawyer, the number of people charged with crimes will increase, so the number of cases will increase. There will be court overcrowding as people are charged and have to go to court. That means that there will be a need for more specialized courts (drug courts) and other diversion programs.

Others in the legal profession reported that the legalization of marijuana would make their lives easier. There would be less work and fewer constitutional issues to think about, especially for issues pertaining to search and seizure. "Of course, there will still be cases on marijuana DUI and other offenses like that. Moreover, legalization would free up police resources. They would not be spending time on finding pot smokers or those who are possessing marijuana."

Some attorneys agreed that when marijuana becomes legal, people probably won't use much more than they currently use. The people who want to use marijuana are using it already. There may be some people who want to try it but do not because they are "super law abiding." These people will try it if it is legal. Further, those people who use marijuana frequently probably will not buy it more often. They often cannot hold jobs and won't have the money to buy it legally, so they either will buy it illegally where it is cheaper or resort to crime as they do now. But, on the whole, this professional did not expect the number of users to increase after legalization.

One professional explained that the system receives a lot of money in fines from people who are guilty of possessing marijuana. If it is legal, they won't get that money any more. But at the same time, there will be other crimes for which people will have to pay fines, so that will probably replace the revenue from "lost" fines.

One lawyer mentioned the impact marijuana legalization could have on police behavior, explaining that police sometimes use drugs as an excuse to enter and search a place. "Smelling dope" can be used as a reason for officers to search cars or homes, even if they are looking for something else. Police use the odor of marijuana as an excuse to give them probable cause for a search. Legalizing marijuana closes that option for cops.

A note made by one professional clarified the role of an attorney with regard to clients. He explained that if someone comes to him to ask how to set up a marijuana-related business, he can advise them because it is now legal in Ohio. Before the law was passed, he could not answer questions because marijuana was illegal. If someone asks how to avoid the law, he cannot give advice to that person. He noted, "I can't help them break the law."

One prosecutor noted that his job was funded by a grant related to the War on Drugs. If there is no longer a War on Drugs, some agencies would lose funding and some people would lose their jobs. As he described it, the War on Drugs has become part of the prison industry complex, and it is used as a way to fill prisons and jails to keep corrections officials employed.

A judge noted that "I will have more people in my court who need drug treatment. There will be more people who end up here after smoking and doing something they don't mean to do or something else crazy and get arrested. Just because it is legal doesn't mean people won't get arrested for drugs any more. Remember that we have other drugs that are causing problems. People will smoke and drive or smoke and beat their wife and end up getting arrested."

Is Marijuana a Gateway Drug?

Many professionals in the legal field do not believe that marijuana is a gateway drug. As one person explained clearly, his belief is that people do not use marijuana then try harder drugs. Some who try weed want to try other drugs, but in the end, it is not a gateway drug. "Marijuana users do not get arrested for other charges. Those who drink alcohol are charged with many offenses—possession, DUI, habitual drunk, maybe property crimes. But marijuana users don't get multiple charges. They don't typically return to court for other drug offenses. They may return for another marijuana charge but not for charges related to other drugs."

One legal professional explained that if you are prone to addictive behavior, then you are likely to become addicted to something in your lifetime. "That can be food, alcohol, or shopping. But marijuana does not cause people to take more drugs."

One professional put a condition on the gateway theory. He stated that marijuana is a gateway drug but only as long as it remains illegal. If legal dispensaries are established, then the black market for marijuana will be cut off, along with access to worse, harder drugs. Legalization will lead to fewer people using harder drugs. They will use more marijuana instead.

Another particularly interesting response implied that marijuana generally is not a gateway drug. "Having said that—if you make this a geographical or socioeconomic question, my answer might change. Is marijuana a gateway drug in suburbia where a person is using it while he/she is undergoing chemo treatment—no. Is marijuana a gateway drug in an urban, gang-infested neighborhood—perhaps it is more likely. It depends on why the person is using marijuana. So if the marijuana is used for medical reasons, the person will probably not use other drugs; if it is used for recreation, then probably yes."

Another reaction to the question was based on the supposition that marijuana is addictive. People who use it, especially if they use it a lot, will experience urges to continue using it. And they have withdrawal symptoms if they do not use soon. In this sense, marijuana is a gateway drug.

Should Medical Marijuana Be Legal?

When it comes to professionals in the legal field, there is a mix of those who support medical marijuana and those who do not. Of those who support it, many noted the medical benefits. It was pointed out that marijuana can be used to treat people who are addicted to heroin. "I feel that it is a viable, nonaddictive option for pain management." As one person said, "If I was sick, sure, I'd try it. Why not?" The negative effects are no worse than other legal substances like tobacco and alcohol, and the possible benefits far outweigh any possible harms.

One legal professional suggested that marijuana should be allowed. He questioned why we spend a lot of money prosecuting it. "It becomes a waste of money. We have other, more pressing needs. If someone can go to a concert and drink as a form of relaxation or escape, why not have a joint? It's the same thing."

Not surprisingly, other legal professionals argued that marijuana should be permitted for both medical and recreational reasons primarily because of the profit. One professional said, "look at Colorado. They are enjoying lots of profits from sale of marijuana. Of course it would have to be regulated (who can sell it and how much and who can smoke it). But it can make a lot of money because it is an untapped revenue stream for the state that can make millions to help with our budget. The revenue can go for transportation, infrastructure, and public schools. We need to find a way to make more money for these areas and taxing marijuana can make a lot of money, like in Colorado."

Those in the legal field who do not support medical marijuana suggest that there are prescription drugs to treat people who are ill, so people should use them. "The drugs are regulated, and we know what they will do to a person's body. You never know what effect the marijuana will have because there is a different dosage every time you use it." For that reason, this professional said he would never use it himself.

Another professional pointed out that there is no evidence to prove that marijuana can treat illnesses, even though lots of people say it can. He went on to say that the only reason marijuana is legal is because a lot of people will make a lot of money from it. One person noted that "we need to either legalize both medical and recreational or neither. It should all be legal; otherwise it gets too confusing and muddled over who can have it and who cannot. The enforcement becomes too difficult."

Even though legal professionals are faced with the issue of marijuana often, many are still unsure about the legalization. "I don't know if it should be legal or not. People say there are benefits to using it, but I don't

know if it is true. The bottom line is that it is illegal: the law says it is illegal. If people are caught with it, possession, or using it, then they should
be sentenced for that. If the law changes, then they won't be sentenced."

Should Recreational Marijuana Be Legal?

A professional in the legal field claims to support the legalization of recreational marijuana "because it is no worse than alcohol or tobacco. People
can get really sick from drinking or smoking cigarettes. Marijuana can't
be worse than those substances."

The legalization of marijuana was likened to alcohol by one respondent. He said, "people won't stop using it. People want to use drugs. It
is like Prohibition. People wanted to drink and found ways to do it. The
violence resulted after we made it illegal. There was so much violence
that we had to legalize it again; now there is little; the same pattern holds
true for marijuana."

"Marijuana should not be legal. It isn't a good choice and many people
do crazy things after using it. We get many people in the system who do
things while they are high that they wouldn't have done if they were not
using and were thinking clearly. They steal things or beat someone up
because they are high. Legalizing marijuana will make it more accessible
to people. Some people may be able to use it and be OK the next day, but
a lot of users can't do that. A lot of people get addicted to marijuana."

This respondent added, "if recreational [marijuana] is passed, this will
become worse, depending on how the law is written. There may be tons
of dispensaries as a way to prevent people from growing their own. Some
laws specify that people can grow their own if there are no dispensaries
within a few miles, so local legislators are forced to pass laws allowing
for dispensaries in their local areas even though they don't want to do that.
They don't want dispensaries in their local areas but a dispensary is better
than having lots of pot plants growing around the neighborhood. It would
be too easy for kids to get to them."

One participant said the following about recreational marijuana: "They
say it isn't addictive but for some people it is. They can't stop using it.
They commit crimes to get more. Then they end up committing some
crime and end up here [in court]. We have that drug [diversion] program
that is really good. It has a high success rate for anyone who graduates.

They learn that it is better to stay off drugs and that they can't use at all. But they have to learn that. And it takes a lot of time for some people. If we legalize it, there will be more people who need to be in that program, and we just can't take many more. There are so many people now who want to go in, and the waiting time to get in can be months. We can't make people wait months to get help. But what else can we do? It's not a good thing."

What Should a Marijuana Law Entail?

One professional argued that doctors should be allowed to prescribe medical marijuana to their clients but only in limited circumstances; for example, if patients have cancer and are in a lot of pain or if they have lost their appetite. The concern that it may become easy to get a prescription for marijuana even though a person is not sick was raised. "I feel that . . . if a person goes to the doctor with a stubbed toe, they can get a medical marijuana card. Young people have access to marijuana when they say they are sick but they really aren't. There has to be more oversight of doctors who give prescriptions for marijuana for no reason."

Another legal professional answered, "I can't say what the law should be, but I know what it is. Whether I agree with it or not doesn't matter. I don't make the laws—other people do that. When offenders appear in front of me and give me a sob story or tell me why they had the drug on them—and most often it is not their fault—I really can't care about that. If they were possessing, then they were guilty, and I have to sentence them for it. Bottom line. Now if the state makes it legal, those people who were already sentenced won't be affected. It will only be cases from that point on. But the state will make new laws about marijuana and people will probably violate those laws."

A different response was provided by another legal professional. He said, "Chances are, the law won't change. But the pharmaceutical companies are probably fighting legalization because they know they have a lot to lose when it comes to profits. If the laws change, people will be using marijuana when they used to turn to pharmaceuticals."

The potential for constitutional issues was noted by one legal professional. He related the concern that there is no test for driving under the influence of marijuana, nor a standard to know when someone is impaired.

"This means that people will be charged with driving under the influence without any way to prove [it]. The police have to use other clues to know if they are high, things like weaving in traffic, driving too slow or too fast. But that could also be a sign that they are texting. It is easy to get off because there is no evidence. The defense can easily get the charges dropped or reduced."

Another lawyer noted something similar. "Scientists from labs are often brought into court to give expert testimony in cases about [whether] a person was under the influence of a drug, but they often cannot give the courts the information they need. Even the scientists do not know the level at which a person is high. It isn't like a DUI at .08 right now. We are getting there, but even once that is set, there will probably be changes. A DUI level used to be higher but then they lowered it."

Other notable comments from legal professionals include those listed in box 6.2.

EDUCATORS

People in the field of education were, in general, concerned about the impact of legalization on the education system. The educators included in the study worked in the field between six and thirty-five years. They included teachers, administrators, and teachers' aides. The people in this group were from a variety of states, including Colorado, Texas, Ohio, and Virginia.

How Will Legalized Marijuana Affect Your Job?

Although some educators indicated that legalized marijuana would not affect their jobs at all, most were concerned about legalized marijuana. They believe students will be more likely to use marijuana and come to school high. If students are under the influence of marijuana, they are unable to think clearly, are not able to learn, and do not do well in school. One teacher said, "It is hard to teach a kid who is either on drugs or who has been taking drugs." Students who are under the influence can sometimes become disruptive in the classroom. Students who are high can't keep up, yet teachers cannot leave them behind. As teachers, they try to encourage

TEXTBOX 6.2. COMMENTS
FROM LEGAL PROFESSIONALS

- "The government should continue to test marijuana to see if it is as bad as they say. We need less addiction pain medications—too many people get hooked on those too often. Marijuana can be used to comfort the addiction crisis. If we don't give out so many pain meds, then people won't get addicted as much."
- "I think as my generation (millenials) gains political power, and as we get more involved, the number of states that legalize marijuana will increase. Most old people don't want it, but young people do. So as the old people get out of office and young people get in, they will pass laws to legalize it more."
- "My understanding is that though lawful in some states, it is still unlawful to grow, use and sell per federal statute. I think that if medicinal marijuana is permitted – there should only be a handful of doctors per region who can prescribe the medication. If a party seeks a prescription and they are denied, there should be an administrative appeals process. There are too many doctors who just give out marijuana prescriptions to anyone who wants one, whether they are sick or not. The law should be changed to limit the number of doctors who can prescribe it. They should be trained and know how marijuana affects a person, or how much they should use. Patients shouldn't be able to use as much as they want legally. It should be more controlled, like other prescription drugs."
- "If marijuana is approved, either medicinally or recreationally, there need to be testing procedures put in place so folks aren't driving under the influence. We don't have that right now, so people who are high may get away with driving after they use pot. They can easily cause an accident and harm others."
- "The real problem is the kids that use. They see their parents or brothers/sisters use, or their friends. They start using drugs because they think its cool. They don't know any better. If their parents are using, then they think its OK. Once a young person uses it is really hard to stop."

students to learn in class but are unable to do so if students are not drug free.

One professional questioned whether teachers will have to learn to detect if students are high or have used marijuana. She questioned if teachers will become police and then stated that the job of teaching is hard enough as it is. Another teacher admitted that she wouldn't report students for drug use unless it was really bad.

An administrator expressed concern that some students may get prescribed marijuana for medical reasons, but he noted that even these students cannot come to school under the influence. If a student is prescribed medical marijuana, the teachers and staff would not be permitted to administer it. This could become a problem if a student must use it throughout the day. Those schools that carry out drug testing of students and/or athletes may be forced to make exceptions for students who are prescribed marijuana and test positive.

The educators noted that they could be fired if they come to work high (though they are not currently drug tested on a regular basis). One school administrator noted that if marijuana was made legal, he would be afraid that more teachers would come to work with marijuana in their system. At that point, he would be forced to fire anyone who tests positive for drug use, even teachers with a prescription for medical marijuana. This could change depending on how the law is written, but he noted that teachers cannot come to class under the influence. Although medical marijuana may not make people high, it often does. The teachers and employees need to be a role model for students and can't come to class high. The schools may have to drug test even more than they currently do, he noted.

One teacher, thinking of the long term, predicted that if marijuana was legal, more students would probably use it, making it difficult to find a job. They may be unable to pass background checks or drug screening tests. Another teacher said, "Marijuana affects young people's minds permanently."

Is Marijuana a Gateway Drug?

Many educators reported that marijuana is not a gateway drug. As one teacher explained, there is no proof that it leads to the use of other drugs. Most students would stick to marijuana if it was legal. Those who use pot won't turn to heroin. Many people use marijuana and never use anything else—like alcohol, people can use it and not want anything else. Prescription drugs are more of a gateway drug than marijuana.

However, other teachers claim that marijuana is a gateway drug, especially for those people who have an addictive personality. Marijuana users are comfortable using it and want to use other drugs. Another teacher explained that marijuana is readily available and easier to obtain than alcohol, especially for kids. They use it, especially if their friends are using, and they get comfortable using drugs. Once young people try marijuana, they might become curious about other drugs. They want to get really high, so they try something else. It might become easier because they know people who sell it.

Should Medical Marijuana Be Legal?

Many educators believe that marijuana should be legal for medical reasons. They argue that marijuana has clear health benefits and helps many people by easing pain from cancer and other ailments. It can help people who are experiencing the effects of chemo treatments. One teacher noted that marijuana is also holistic/natural so it isn't harmful like many prescription drugs and doesn't have serious side effects. As another teacher said, if people want to try it, why not? "If someone want to use it and it makes them feel better, they should be allowed, particularly for serious cases."

One teacher's personal experience influenced her opinion. She has a son who has seizures and she has considered using marijuana because of research that shows that marijuana helps children who suffer from seizures. She reported that she suffers from back pain and has considered marijuana for herself if it becomes legal. It is one alternative to helping those people who suffer from pain as opposed to using prescription drugs.

Other professionals did not support medical marijuana use. One teacher explained that we do not know the long-term effects of marijuana use, especially on children. Another teacher said, "We should legalize medical marijuana if someone is really sick, but not for people who say they have a headache. A lot of doctors recommend it for backaches or something that doesn't exist, especially to young people. They just want to get high legally. But if someone has terminal cancer and is in a lot of pain, then they should be allowed to use whatever drug makes them comfortable."

Should Recreational Marijuana Be Legal?

The majority of teachers felt that marijuana should not be legalized for either medical or recreational reasons. They explained that if marijuana was legal, it would be too easy for students to get and they would more than likely use it. Too many students currently come to school high and can't learn. Plus, legalized marijuana may lead to more injuries; for example, someone driving while high. One teacher said that marijuana should not be legal for recreational reasons because it is too dangerous for children.

Other teachers felt that we should legalize recreational marijuana. They pointed to data that shows that locking up a person for marijuana offenses is costly. Plus, there are far worse criminal offenders who should be locked up but aren't because prison overcrowding. Finally, it was argued that marijuana it is not addictive and therefore should be legal.

A teacher made the argument that it is common for teachers to tell students not to smoke tobacco, so why not speak against smoking pot? He said that "we've worked for years to reduce tobacco smoking, so why are we encouraging smoking another drug? Any time you put smoke into your lungs, it will affect the body, so why is smoke from marijuana different from smoke from tobacco? If we make marijuana legal, there will have to be lots of programs to teach kids to not use it. We currently have DARE [Drug Abuse Resistance Education] but it doesn't work so well. We will have to institute more antidrug programs geared toward children at a very young age."

Another person in the profession reported, "I do not think marijuana should be legal. Since it has been legal in Colorado, it seems that more students have come to school high and the students joke around about getting high more often. We should not be encouraging our students and young people to take drugs. I see high people in the stores all the time, and they stink, like they were just smoking in their cars. It may have medical benefits for people who are really sick, but a lot of people who are using it are not sick. They just want to be high. There may be a lot of people making a lot of money from marijuana, but they shouldn't be allowed to make money by ruining people's lives."

Other respondents were ambivalent: "I don't think marijuana should be legal. Legalizing the drug makes it more accessible to people and sends a message that it is OK to use it. I don't think we should be allowing people to take drugs because they really are not good for you. But, at the same time, if someone wants to use a drug, why not? As long as they don't hurt anyone else while they are high—as long as they don't drive or do anything crazy, then why not? But I worry a lot about young people who use the drug. Young people don't know how to control their use. I hate to see young people who are addicted to drugs. Then when they get old, they wish they hadn't used when they were young."

"It's like alcohol. Too much alcohol isn't good for a person and lots of people do stupid things when they are drunk. Even a drink or two every day over a long time isn't healthy. But it is legal anyway. The government taxes it and we make a lot of money. It's harmful but the state lets people use it, as long as they don't drink and drive or hurt someone else. So I guess if we use that logic, marijuana should be legal. But I still don't think it should be."

What Should a Marijuana Law Entail?

One teacher noted that if there is a law that makes marijuana legal, there should be no monopolies. Instead, a person should be able to grow it in their backyard if they want to. Another teacher suggested that a law allowing for legal marijuana should limit who can sell it. That person must get a license and be regulated by the state. An alternative suggestion was to legalize recreational marijuana like we do alcohol. That way, people can use it on Friday nights to relax. Most people won't have a problem using it on occasion and they won't become addicted that quickly.

Many educators indicated that marijuana sales should be taxed. Not surprisingly, many teachers thought that any revenue produced should be spent on schools. One educator noted that in Colorado, the schools don't seem to be getting much money from marijuana taxes. There are lots of schools, so even if there is a lot of money for the state, the individual schools aren't getting much when it's divided up. Other suggestions for using revenue included paying for infrastructure for the state or health care. Another suggestion was to spend the money on agencies that help people, such as nonprofits that help children who have diseases or cancer. Another professional was concerned that there is no test to determine if a person is high. She said, "we have to find a way to figure this out before we make the drug legal."

One educator suggested that growing and using hemp should be legalized because of its strong fiber, which can be used in clothing and for industrial purposes.

One educator's concerns were more complex. He argued that we no longer teach students personal responsibility for their actions, and they are often not held responsible for what they do. He explained that it has become a cultural and moral problem in this country. Many people have lost their moral direction. If we had more people who had a moral or religious base, they wouldn't be searching to fill a void with drugs like marijuana. The government can't fix the lack of moral values through government, but many of our laws are ways to make people have morals. Parents aren't teaching their kids that drugs are bad; many parents are on drugs themselves so they aren't capable of teaching their own kids or acting as role models for their kids.

He continued explaining that if marijuana remains illegal, it is the government's way of saying it is wrong. If parents don't tell kids that using drugs is wrong, then the government has to do it. If they make it legal, then it is like the government is telling kids that it is OK to use drugs.

STUDENTS

Many college-aged students were interviewed about their perspectives on marijuana legalization. Most students were typical college aged (eighteen to twenty-five), but a few were older, nontraditional students. Men and women, both graduate and undergraduate students were included in this study. The students were from many states, including Ohio, Pennsylvania, Florida, and others.

How Will Legalized Marijuana Affect You as a Student?

Many students reported that the legalization of marijuana will not affect them. Some noted that their friends may smoke more if marijuana is made legal, but they will not. But one said that if a person has friends who smoke a lot, the person probably will, too (but if they have friends that are into sports, they will probably not use). Others indicated concern about getting caught using marijuana, since it may affect their prospects of getting jobs in the future. Most of the students noted that they did not foresee an increase in crime resulting from legalization.

One student respondent described how marijuana use affected his current job at a rental car company. He explained that people rent a car and then fill the car with marijuana smoke because it purportedly gets people high more quickly as compared to other ways of ingesting it. The odor from the smoke gets into the upholstery and the carpeting, and although the rental company employees try to get the smell out, they are unable to do so. The person who rented the car is fined $150.

Student opinions were split as to whether marijuana use causes crime. Some believed that marijuana use does not lead to crime, nor does it lead people to commit robberies like other drugs do. Moreover, if marijuana is legalized, crime will not increase—it may even decrease because people who are arrested for use or possession now won't be arrested anymore. No study has shown that it causes crime, as one student said. On the other hand, one student said that there is no doubt that marijuana use leads to more crime. "Drugs equal crime. People commit crime to get money to buy more drugs."

Is Marijuana a Gateway Drug?

Many students indicated that marijuana is not a gateway drug. They described how many people use marijuana but do not use other drugs. It was noted that people who use alcohol or cigarettes are more likely to turn to other drugs than people who use pot. One student claimed that it has been factually proven not to be a gateway drug.

Some students said that marijuana is not addictive, but others said that it can be addictive for those who have an obsessive personality or for those who have used drugs in the past. One student described the emotional addiction to marijuana that some users have, explaining that emotional addiction is sometimes worse than physical addiction.

Conversely, one student said that marijuana is a gateway drug. He explained that some users who smoke large quantities of weed are more likely to try other illegal drugs. Other students indicated that users want to try other, more harmful drugs after they use marijuana. As one student said, "It starts with marijuana and then leads people to take other drugs." Another stated, "I believe that any recreational substance that is not prescribed in a regulated manner from a recognized doctor can lower inhibitions and lead to taking chances and trying things one might not otherwise try. So they may be more likely to use other drugs. . . . People get used to the feeling of being high and want to try another drug, or maybe someone offers it to them, and since they are used to using drugs, they will try something new."

Should Medical Marijuana Be Legal?

Many students reported that medical marijuana should be legal. Their responses are provided in box 6.3.

TEXTBOX 6.3.   STUDENT RESPONSES

- "Because it helps people feel better (which was based on what the scientists say and they know more than I). I would smoke it if a doctor said so or prescribed it."
- "It is just a plant and there is nothing wrong with it."
- "It has been used for patients who have cerebral palsy and epilepsy and really bad forms of autism. I would use it if a doctor gave it to me."
- "Marijuana has been proven through science to be useful for medical conditions such as chronic pain, appetite stimulation for cancer patients and chemo; insomnia, Alzheimer's disease, and the list goes on."
- "It can be used as a substitution for more dangerous drugs like opioids. In some states, doctors prescribe marijuana instead of opioids. Marijuana is less addictive and less dangerous."
- "It is less addictive than opioids and I wouldn't want to get addicted. You are less likely to get addicted to marijuana after treatment."
- "Marijuana has proven benefits in managing pain with few side effects. It is much easier for the body to digest and since it is natural there are not many unintended medical effects."

- "Medical marijuana has benefits for people who are sick. It can help to reduce pain in some people and help with other ailments. Sick people should be allowed to choose to use it if they want."
- "We should not criminalize medicine. If someone is sick and needs to have this drug to get better, then they should be able to use it and have access to it."
- "I smoke it and love it so why not let sick people? They will feel better after using it."
- "There are no good reasons to keep it illegal."
- "Medical marijuana should be legal because we have 4 generations of marijuana research showing that its safer than alcohol."
- "It is beneficial for medical purposes."
- "It reduces pain for patients who have terminal illnesses or chronic pain. They can avoid taking oxycontin or other opioids that are really addicting."
- "People with preexisting conditions are being prosecuted for a means of medical treatment and they shouldn't be. If it helps them deal with their medical problems, and it is prescribed by a doctor, they should be allowed to use it."
- "People are going to use it anyway so it might as well be legal so we can tax it and get a lot of money. They say it has the power to help people with some medical conditions. I don't know if it is true but like I said, they are going to use it. Lots of people use it now medically even though it is illegal."
- "It should be legal for the tax revenue. We can make an enormous amount of tax money and then we can reduce taxes on other things that shouldn't be taxed."
- "It can be safer if it is legal."
- "It is no worse than any other drugs that people use. Some drugs that are prescribed by doctors have serious medical side effects, some of which can last a long time or be permanent. Marijuana does not have that effect on people. For the most part, it has no side effects for users."

A few students indicated that medical marijuana should not be legal. They explained that some people may use marijuana for medical reasons and then decide that they like it and then use it for other reasons. Another agreed that it should be legal but only if used in hospitals. He said, "People shouldn't be able to grow it themselves. You don't know the strength of the marijuana."

Should Recreational Marijuana Be Legal?

Many students suggested that recreational marijuana should be legal for the potential tax revenue, noting that some states have emerged from serious tax deficits because of selling and taxing marijuana. Another reason for legalizing recreational marijuana is that people may use it and not turn to other drugs like heroin, which can kill them. One student noted that he would like to walk in the park and feel free to smoke outside (which would be banned under most state laws). One student used the legalization of marijuana to argue for less government involvement in people's lives. He said that the government shouldn't say what people can and cannot do. Another suggested that if marijuana was legal, it would be safer.

A response indicated that people should not support putting people in a cage [i.e., a jail cell] because they have a dried plant. Further, freeing people convicted of possession of marijuana would reduce the prison population, also saving money. Those released from prison then would be required to hold jobs so that they will be paying taxes. "Most users are mellow and want to have fun," explained one person. "Why not let people have fun after a hard day?"

A few students felt that recreational marijuana should not be legal. One has a relative who is a paramedic and sees the dangers of drug use. Another reported watching marijuana "destroy the motivation of my niece to the point that she has no goals or ambition. People who smoke marijuana regularly lose part of their brain or something and they don't want to have a job or go to school. They just get lazy and don't want to work. They just want to smoke more."

Although many students agreed that recreational marijuana should be legal, some also placed limits on it. For example, one respondent said that marijuana should not be used by people in professions such as teaching or law enforcement or by those who operate heavy machinery, such as airplanes, which require quick reflexes. "Someone who smokes marijuana won't be able to focus on what they need to do. People whose jobs require concentration and thinking can't smoke marijuana. It makes your brain too foggy." Another person said, "I have never seen a single case where it motivates people to be better."

One student wrote of being "on the fence" about the legalization of recreational marijuana. On one hand, it was not uncommon for students to say, "why should I care if others use marijuana?" On the other hand, some students noted that legalization is likely an irreversible decision, and "there are still health and societal problems that could arise or even become worse with the legalization of recreational marijuana."

What Should a Marijuana Law Entail?

According to many students, a law legalizing marijuana should put money from taxes toward DARE programs, which teach kids to stay away from drugs. Other students proposed that the revenue should be allocated for drug rehab programs for people who are addicted to any drug. Another suggested that marijuana taxes should help fund schools.

Another person wanted to see limits on marijuana advertising. Advertising should be discreet or not allowed at all. This would be a way of protecting kids from seeing it, which would only normalize marijuana use for them.

Some students felt that if marijuana was made legal, it should be regulated much like alcohol or tobacco. There should be regulations on the amount one can buy. Also, the government should oversee growers and distributors through a permit system, for example.

Student respondents had many other comments about the legalization of marijuana. These are included in box 6.4.

CONCLUSION

Law enforcement officers seem to have mixed opinions when it comes to the legalization of marijuana. They often must deal with people who have used drugs, so they are fully aware of the potential dangers of drugs. Although many people can use marijuana safely, others may react differ-

TEXTBOX 6.4.   STUDENT COMMENTS

- "My managers at work (a restaurant) get high all the time. The servers get high before, during and after work. None of the customers know."
- "Marijuana was legal for a long time. It was only made illegal because of racism. All the founding fathers smoked dope."
- "Lots of my friends smoke."
- "The government can't stop people from using it."
- "My friend's grandmother uses it. She gets it in the mail from a person in Colorado."
- "My mom works in the post office and lots of packages smell like pot but they don't do anything about it."
- "Its so easy to get marijuana even in illegal states."
- "Most people only get caught if they smoke in public. Even then cops don't do anything. It can be an "add on" so if you are caught doing something else then they add on an extra charge."
- "If it was legal I would try it."
- "It will come up in a social situation if it became legal."
- "Because use is so high rate, making it illegal doesn't stop. The penalties are so inconsequential."
- "A lot of my friends in engineering are drug tested. They hold sensitive jobs."
- "The government should continue to do testing on marijuana so we know more about the medical benefits. Then we can also know how to regulate it."
- "In the next few years, I think marijuana will become more widely legalized. More states will allow it. More people accept its use now and they will vote for it."
- "In the next few years, the federal government is likely to oppose legal marijuana under the Republicans. More states are likely to at least decriminalize, if not legalize, the drug; if another president is elected in four years, then there may be a better chance of it becoming legal federally."

- "I think its abundantly clear that we know that marijuana is safe. It is not made legal because of politics and because of money. It costs too much money to make it legal."
- "It will become legal on the federal level when democrats are in power."
- "I think lawyers and other professionals would get a lot more done if they would get blazed on the weekends. They'd be more relaxed on Monday morning."
- "If marijuana is legal, the economy will get better. More people will buy it and the money will go back into the economy."
- "The government should continue testing marijuana: they may find that it is a legitimate pain reliever and it could help in other areas such as NFL players who are in pain."
- "More drugs exist than just pot, so we need to think about more than just pot. Pot really isn't the issue. The problem is heroin and its effect. We need to put more attention and money into that than pot."
- "In the next 5–10 years it will become legal. This is unfortunate because it will lead society to be lazy."
- "If it were legal, I may use the drug just to try it. I've never used it before. I would not make it a habit, though, because I think it affects people's brains. They can't think clearly if they use it a lot and for a long time."
- "In the next few years, there will be total legalization. It's the new 'gay marriage.' Everyone will be OK with it eventually."

ently. Professionals in the legal field also witness the consequences of marijuana use, but at the same time, they recognize that legalization may provide more clients. Educators have special concerns about marijuana legalization since they are focused on educating young people who may be less likely to succeed academically if they choose to experiment with marijuana. At the same time, school administrators must also consider personnel issues pertaining to possible use by teachers and other personnel. As a group, students understand that there are dangers associated with the legalization of marijuana but seem to be more accepting of its use.

Chapter Seven

A Professional
and Political Perspective

This chapter continues to describe how members of different professions view the legalization of marijuana. The people interviewed for this chapter were more diverse, so their stories are told in smaller vignettes. Respondents include international representatives, professionals in the marijuana industry, and politicians.

INTERNATIONAL RESPONDENTS

A limited number of international respondents were included in this study. Most were young, but one respondent was in his fifties. The sample included both men and women. They represented Ghana, Canada, and South Korea.

Ghana

Marijuana is illegal in Ghana for both medical and recreational use, so not many people use it. Those who use it and are caught are sent to jail for a year, even for only a small amount. In schools, young people are told that marijuana causes mental problems, though it is easy to obtain in high schools.

People who live in Ghana do not think about legalizing marijuana, said one respondent. The United Nations said it should be legal, he thinks for medical reasons, as well as hemp. One respondent from Ghana did not support marijuana legalization for medical reasons. If he was sick, he

would use it only if there was proof that it worked, but right now there is
no real proof that it works to cure diseases. Another respondent explained
that marijuana should not be legal because it causes mental problems.
He knows many people who use and who have mental problems. Their
behavior is different after using. However, he did point out that the marijuana in Africa is stronger because of the climate.

One respondent said that marijuana is not a gateway drug since it does
not make people use harder drugs; another participant disagreed, saying
that marijuana is a gateway drug because it makes a person take other
drugs.

Canada

Marijuana was legal in Canada for a while. Parliament passed a law so
now the government health care system uses marijuana for some medical
conditions. The participant agrees that medical marijuana should be legal.
There are many types of marijuana that people could use. If it helps a sick
person feel better, then they should be able to use it. Prescription drugs
don't always work the way we want them to; they can have bad side effects. People should have marijuana as an option.

Recreational marijuana should also be legal, according to this participant. Marijuana use is no different than alcohol. People should be able to
use it on a Friday night and then not use it again for a while.

A law legalizing marijuana should have multiple checks and regulations. Legislators should ensure that it is not being sold on the black market and that the laws are being followed.

South Korea

The participant explained that Koreans don't think about marijuana the
way they do in the United States. It is rare for anyone to use marijuana or
other illegal drugs in South Korea—most people don't even think about
it. They do not have programs like DARE, because there is no need to
teach kids to not use marijuana. The respondent wasn't sure what would
happen if someone was caught with marijuana, but she assumed that he
or she would probably go to jail. The thought of legalizing marijuana isn't
even considered. Given that, the respondent didn't believe that marijuana

should be legal in South Korea for either recreational or medical use any time soon.

This participant believed that marijuana probably is a gateway drug and that people will want to take more drugs if they use marijuana. But she then clarified that by saying that her perception is probably based on what she was taught in school as a young child.

MARIJUANA INDUSTRY

Four respondents in the study worked in the marijuana industry in some capacity. It is a growing industry with a great deal of risk and uncertainty for investors, business owners, and employees. Two of the respondents were in their twenties, one was in his forties. There were both male and female respondents.

Investor

One participant was a male in his forties who had been working on Wall Street in New York as an investor but did not see much of a future in his job. He explained that his job was hectic with lots of stress. He didn't like the firm he was with, so he left the company to become a marijuana tester. He and his wife and kids moved to Los Angeles, California, where the industry is less regulated than in Colorado. The respondent and his friends are working on developing a marijuana testing service. So far, the respondent enjoys working in the industry. He described the people in the industry as generally nice, his income is higher, and he isn't under so much stress.

At this point, this professional is not worried about the government shutting everything down—the marijuana industry is too large for that to happen. He explained that even if President Trump or Attorney General Sessions cracks down on marijuana, they will not be able to dismantle the entire industry. There are just too many people who want to use the drug. One indicator of that is the success of marijuana stores and companies. He predicted that marijuana will become legal across the nation in the next few years. Even if President Trump does not sign a law to legalize it, maybe the next president will.

Container Salesperson 1

Another participant was a twenty-year-old male who just had started a job selling sealable containers that can be used to transport marijuana safely. He reported that he enjoys his job and working in the industry. He likes the product, so he likes to sell it. The container is odor proof and prevents drug dogs from smelling marijuana contained within it. As for predicting the future of the marijuana industry, he was unable to say with any certainty what might happen. He felt certain that the president could "take this all away." He explained that many states have made marijuana legal, so the president couldn't change that. On the other hand, this is just a job to him, one that is more fun than working at McDonalds or at the mall. Thus, if the president did make it illegal, he would get another job—it's no real big deal to him.

Container Salesperson 2

The third participant was a twenty-year-old male who sells large plastic containers used to transport marijuana. He travels a lot for his job, and although he is used to the travel and likes it, it can also be tiring. Many of his friends take edibles such as cookies and candies on planes when they travel, and they have never been caught by security or even by drug dogs. A possible explanation for this is that the scent of the food masks the scent of the drug. He also has many friends who mail marijuana to themselves or others and have never been caught, something that he's never done because he doesn't want to get caught. Since marijuana is easy to buy nearly anywhere you go, it isn't worth the risk to try to put it in the mail. This respondent believes the industry will only continue to grow in the future. He points to the success of the "massive" marijuana conferences, particularly in Los Angeles, where there are about five hundred exhibitors and thousands of participants. President Trump can try to fight legalization, but he won't succeed. He wouldn't have enough money to go after all of the companies and the people who want to use marijuana. Even though it is illegal, people still use it, and the government won't be able to stop it. The government may as well make it all legal and get the money from it.

University Faculty

The fourth respondent was an untenured university chemistry professor who works at a university that is offering a new degree in chemistry to teach students how to test marijuana plants for potency. However, students will not be permitted to grow marijuana, since only the University of Mississippi legally can grow marijuana plants for the federal government's testing program. The respondent's school has applied for permission to grow plants but has not received a response from the government. Instead, the students will test other plants, since the process for testing is the same. He thinks the industry will become legal in the future and more people will get involved in it. It is big business with a lot of money to be made.

Lawyer

The fifth respondent from the marijuana industry is a young lawyer who recently graduated from law school and now works at a law firm based in New York. The firm advises people who are active in the marijuana industry. The New York Supreme Court made a decision to allow lawyers to advise clients in the marijuana industry on business-related matters, but they are not permitted to help clients break the law or they could be reported to the New York State bar and punished through them. For the most part, this participant enjoys advising clients in this field. There are few attorneys who specialize in this area, so there is a lot of business. There are many unknowns and the field is constantly changing, which makes it interesting. His clients have companies that are like any other companies. Much of what he does is simply business-related law, since his clients have many of the same questions that any other company owner would have, although there are questions that don't pertain to other companies.

Extractor Equipment Sales

An older female participant sells equipment that extracts THC from marijuana leaves. She enjoys selling the product because she gets to meet a lot of new people from many parts of the country. She sells a good product that she believes in. The participant believes that marijuana can help a lot of people with different medical conditions and should be legal. That way it can be regulated and consumers can get the best product possible.

Lighting Salesman

Another participant was an older male in his late sixties who sold lighting for marijuana growers. Although he enjoyed what he did, he was ready to leave his job. He explained that there are many developments in the field and no one knows what the best kind of lighting should be at this time—it is still experimental. He knows the field will develop quickly in the next few years as more is learned about the product. His job was driven completely by the needs of the consumer. There was too much uncertainty in the field for his taste.

Odorless Bags Sales

A male in his mid-thirties, this participant has made a lot of money selling bags that obscure the odor of marijuana. Users can carry marijuana on planes in the bags without detection. This participant has been selling the product for eight years and the company is doing very well, making good profits. He predicts that the industry will only continue to grow, which will open up new and great opportunities for him. He doesn't see himself moving into another part of the industry; he wants to stay in his current job. People will always have a need to buy bags to transport their product. He reported that the government may as well make marijuana legal and raise money from taxes. It would be impossible to arrest everyone who uses.

Light Sales

This study participant sells lighting to marijuana growers. He believes that marijuana should be legal because it would translate into more business for him. In the future, most marijuana will be highly regulated in terms of mold or insects on the plants, meaning that most large grow operations will have to grow inside (outside grow sites have too many bugs). Moreover, the weather can be too unpredictable to grow outside—there may be too many cloudy or rainy days. He agrees that state officials should regulate how the plant is grown. It needs to be safe so users don't get sick. Users cannot be inhaling mold. He believes that marijuana is good for people and fixes all kinds of ailments without make them sicker like other drugs. It also doesn't make you hungover like alcohol. In the near future, most states will make it legal and it will become a crop like strawberries or tomatoes.

Possible Investor

A possible investor (an architect) from a southern state was unsure if marijuana should be legal. He admitted that some people say it has medical benefits, but he wasn't sure because he has never used it. But he knew it was going to be legal in his state soon and was considering investing a large amount of money into some aspect of the field. He was concerned that there may be more crime or more people doing stupid things because they're high. But if the legislature says it's OK, then that's the law. He assumed that a lot of people have made a lot of money in the industry, but he was worried about a crackdown by the federal government and President Trump. If that happens, he could lose his money. But he thought that getting into the industry now may be a good thing for an investor—there was a lot of money to be made.

POLITICIANS

State Rep (Democrat)

This politician believed that medical marijuana should be legal. Most states will have specific rules to oversee the implementation of legal marijuana. Those who are issued a license to grow marijuana must show that they have enough money and a viable plan to carry out the grow operation properly. Anyone in the field right now runs the risk of losing money. Growing marijuana is difficult to do, and it is still illegal by the federal government. An investor could make millions or lose it all. Even if marijuana is legal, it will be highly regulated like alcohol. The black market will still exist, and there's not much the state can do about that. It is better that the law is made by the legislators rather than through a referendum by the voters, because the legislators can control the content of the law. If approved by the voters, it becomes an amendment to the state constitution, which is very difficult to pass.

City Manager (Republican)

Legalized marijuana is a concern to this city manager of a small city because he will have to monitor drug testing more closely. The employees of the city are now drug tested and can be fired if they test positive for drugs. Whether this will happen more if marijuana is legalized depends in part on how the law is written. If an employee has a prescription for medical marijuana, they may not be automatically fired—it all depends on how the law is written. Certainly employees cannot come to work high, prescription or not. They may have to use traditional drugs to treat illnesses.

As a city manager, this respondent may have to regulate dispensaries if the city wants them. The city council will have to decide whether to allow dispensaries within the city, and if so, where they will be located, how many there will be, who will own them, and how to regulate them. The law will probably not be clear on those questions.

Interest Group Lobbyist

A professional political advocate in an area not related to marijuana said that the organization does not recognize marijuana as a problem that needs their full attention. The use of marijuana is still illegal federally, so the organization is not becoming involved in the topic. The organization polls their membership and constituents regularly and marijuana never has been identified as an issue for them. In the course of their polls, they discovered that many older people in Colorado are selling their homes as they downsize or move into retirement homes. These houses are then turned into marijuana grow sites. Buyers install the equipment needed to grow large quantities of pot, do that for a short time, and then move out before they are caught. This largely ruins the house. In fact, quite a few have blown up or burned down because of the heat and chemicals used. The marijuana that is sold is illegally exported to four surrounding states.

Congressional Legislative Aide (Democrat)

An aide for a member of U.S. Congress explained that the congressman was, at the time of this survey, still reviewing this issue but explained further that he is in favor of legalizing medical marijuana. What is unknown to him is the best way to regulate medical marijuana. He plans to take a close look at Washington and Colorado to see how it is working there. He feels that marijuana is a gateway to heroin and other drugs. He is more concerned about the heroin epidemic than marijuana.

Polling Agency

One employee at a polling agency located in Washington, D.C., said that most polls show an overwhelming level of support for medical marijuana. Public opinion continues to change quickly in this area, and we've seen a dramatic change in the number of people who support marijuana legalization. Most people younger than fifty support it and those older than fifty do not. Recreational marijuana is much more controversial than medical. Chances are that the federal government probably won't make it legal anytime soon. Politics will get in the way. The bigger question is whether the feds will start cracking down on those states that have legalized it.

Conservative Think Tank

Members of this national organization said that the issue of marijuana legalization has not been an issue that they have considered or taken any action on. It is not, at this point, a significant social issue that has been identified on their research agenda.

Senator (Republican)

A republican U.S. senator agrees that medical marijuana is acceptable but recreational marijuana is not. He believes that marijuana is a gateway drug. Proof of that came from personal interviews with one thousand people about their drug use, and many of whom told him that they started smoking dope in high school and went on to use harder drugs. The focus should be on treatment and recovery for those who use it and teaching kids that it is not OK to use marijuana. Legalizing it gives the impression it is OK.

Staff Worker for State Attorney General

According to one staff worker in the state attorney general's office, legalized marijuana will add a whole new level to the opioid problem and make it worse. According to this respondent, marijuana is definitely a gateway drug and people who use pot will use harder drugs. The fact that it is a gateway drug has been proven. It has also been proven that people get addicted to pot. When you use it a lot, you keep using it. We need to keep kids from using marijuana so that they do not turn to opioids. The cartels are bringing pot into the United States, not just to Arizona or other border states. They are bringing it to all states and selling it, and the pot they are selling is much stronger than it used to be, which is part of the addiction problem. When kids (and others) use marijuana, they then reach for heroin. It's a serious problem. We need to focus on prevention rather than treatment. Treatment is important but we really need to stop drug use before it starts.

Miscellaneous

A hotel worker in Denver explained that legalized marijuana causes hotels trouble because visitors come to Denver to smoke pot. More than likely, they will smoke in the rooms, and many smoke a large quantity or smoke often. When they leave, the room smells like marijuana, a smell that is difficult to eliminate. The hotel workers will often leave the room door open, sometimes even with fans on, and use room deodorizing spray. There have been times where it has been so bad that the hotel was forced to buy new furnishings (mattresses, bedding, curtains, etc.). This has happened more frequently since recreational marijuana was made legal.

A business owner in Colorado had a different perspective. He struggled with drug testing his employees given that marijuana was legal in the state. At his company, he is required to fill out paperwork and take employees who come to work high or are suspected of being high to a facility for a drug test. If an employee fails a drug test, refuses to take a drug test, or refuses to complete rehab class, he or she is automatically fired by the union. To the business owner, that means that he is short an employee and is forced to hire and/or train someone else for the position. Although he doesn't want people who are using drugs in the company, it will become difficult to keep losing employees for drug use.

He explained further that employees are not permitted to use medicinal marijuana on the job site, even though it is legal. The job is too dangerous to risk a person being high, even though medical marijuana is not supposed to have that effect. Further, the company abides by a drug-free workplace policy in order to take advantage of cheaper rates on workman's compensation insurance.

A retired man in Ohio had some interesting things to say about the legalization of marijuana. First, the man explained variations in enforcement this way: Obama smoked marijuana, so he didn't want to enforce the laws. On the other hand, Trump has not used marijuana, so he's going to enforce the laws. Further, this man explained that he was raised in the country, so he doesn't use the drug. Conversely, he explained, if you were raised in the city, then you would be more likely to use it.

This man said that there is too much peer pressure for kids to use drugs today. Many young people don't care what they do to their bodies. They don't know what they are doing to their bodies. They don't listen to older people who tell them not to smoke or not to do drugs.

He also linked marijuana use to unemployment. He explained that if people don't work, they become depressed and are more likely to use drugs. Additionally, if a family doesn't have a person who earns a regular paycheck, they are more likely to use drugs. He explained that if you have no job, you have no self-esteem. You want to escape your life, so you do drugs. He continued that if the government creates jobs, then drug use will go down. People who are on drugs can't get jobs. One solution is to have drug addicts travel to different schools and talk to kids as part of their treatment or rehabilitation. They can tell kids how bad it is to be addicted and how they lost everything. This way, maybe kids will understand how bad drug use can be.

Another retired man from Ohio took a different perspective. He said that all drugs should be legal because the war against them is not worth it. If people want to use drugs, then why not let them? They are going to use them no matter what the law is. It is natural to do drugs. People have used them for many years. We need to legalize drugs and sell them through legal places. That way it is easier to provide treatment options as well.

Any person who is caught selling drugs on the street should be sentenced to life in prison, according to this retiree. There should be no second chances, no dropping charges. We need to either make drugs legal or very illegal; it's the only way to deal with the problem that makes sense. The penalty for selling drugs must be severe. That way, people will think about using or selling drugs before they actually do it. This is the only way to deter people from using or selling drugs.

This man likened the legalization of marijuana to Prohibition. During Prohibition, people wanted to drink, so organized crime provided alcohol, and the bad guys made all the money. It's the same with marijuana. People want to use it and it is illegal, so the bad guys are providing it and making millions. In addition, they are not punished when they break the law.

An older respondent complained that the United States is losing the War on Drugs. The government spends billions each year to keep kids off drugs, but there are more people using now than ever. There are lots of drugs coming into the country and not enough law enforcement to keep them out. The country needs to have more laws and more severe punishment for those who are selling and trafficking.

This respondent argued that marijuana should be sold in true drugstores and only to those who have a prescription. That way, the pharmacist can track who is buying the drug, for what reason, and how much (or how often). There should also be a licensed clinician who can help people who need marijuana if they become addicted or need further medical care.

CONCLUSION

Members of each of the professions queried have similar though varied perspectives on the legalization of marijuana. Each profession has a wide variety of ideas and predictions about how legalization will affect their jobs, some predicting no impact, while others foresee more serious consequences. Similar trends can be found among all of the professions represented here, particularly those regarding possible dangers of marijuana use among young people and the suggestion that marijuana should be made legal for the tax revenue potential. There are many unknowns about these new laws that allow for legal use of marijuana for medical and recreational reasons, and members of all professions must adapt to whatever changes occur.

It is clear that new laws legalizing marijuana are controversial and will continue to be debated. While it is safe to say that public opinion concerning marijuana is becoming more accepting of the drug, there are still many people who oppose the legalization of marijuana. These responses help us understand more about this debate and what the future might hold.

Chapter Eight

The Debate on Legalization

Though gaining insight into specific groups' perspectives on marijuana and its legalization is essential in understanding how society views the topic, it is perhaps more important to understand how individuals within various groups think about the topic of legalization. The following chapters focus on this cross-group analysis, not drawing distinctions based on role or employment, as the earlier chapters did.

This type of analysis allows us to attempt to reconstruct different ways of thinking about marijuana and in turn to relate those ways of thinking to how society tends to view issues of legalization. As such, there are few references to the groups examined in chapters 1 through 7 and a much more focused analysis on the individual level. While a public opinion poll can provide excellent answers to broad questions about what aggregate groups think about marijuana, the approach taken here is meant to draw out more specific and nuanced ways of seeing the issue and to contextualize them across individuals and groups.

This, more than providing an important basis for discussion, also moves our understanding of the debate regarding legalization forward and may impact our understanding of future attempts to legalize other "vices." Thus, it is important to note that although we cannot claim to be representative in our sample, there is no reason to believe that the ideas we uncover in the following chapters are not present in other individuals and groups and at the very least, their discovery here makes further examination—and further discussion—necessary.

A NOTE ON METHOD

Though there are a number of ways to examine data, we have taken a qualitative, inductive approach called grounded theory akin to that suggested by Charmaz.[1] In adopting an approach based on induction, we hope to draw from the data information that already exists—in essence, to help make sense of it beyond the manifest meaning of the speech itself. This is not a single-stage process, and it has developed significantly over the course of the research, with questions in the in-depth interviews probing for additional information about who could be considered an expert and based on what information—and what types of experience—people felt they could rely on. These questions, sometimes direct, were one source of the information gleaned here. Another source were offhand comments within other interview questions, not necessarily directed at the information here. Although often shorter, these sometimes were more enlightening in terms of the overall framework we have developed here.

The flexibility of grounded theory was one of the reasons we felt that its use here was warranted. A second and perhaps more important reason was that we could develop the information and test it as we went. Writing any kind of full text is daunting, but being able to effectively gather, analyze, and interpret the data in a single step has been a significant element within the current analysis, as it has allowed us to go back to participants when necessary to clarify elements or to help us develop new questions for the interviews as the research progressed. Grounded theory itself is designed around this idea of "continuous questioning" and was therefore essential in developing the ideas put forth here.

THREE CONTESTED AREAS OF LEGALIZATION

Although there are many interesting elements within the data, there were three primary topics that may generate particularly interesting discussion. First is the role of knowledge and expertise within the legalization framework. The second is the role of language and metaphor within the context of our understanding of marijuana and legalization. Third is the politics of legalization from the standpoint of broader social problems.

Each of these perspectives provides a different lens through which to view the legalization debate. Far from being exclusive, these lenses can be layered in interesting ways, and in each case additional perspective can be gained through that layering. Moreover, as we have tried to contextualize each of the chapters in the broader literature, the chapters open up new opportunities for exploration and discussion for the reader. As this was the goal, we have avoided seeking "definitive" answers in favor of interesting interpretations, though we also believe these interpretations have value as explanations.

Given the reliance of the debate regarding marijuana legalization—both recreational and medical—on some of the frames we put forth, the cross-cutting analyses provided in the next chapters offer what we hope are not only explanations for different perspectives on legalization and the bases of discussion as a topic, but also more general approaches to other "vices" that may be legalized.

QUALITATIVE ASSESSMENT

One thing the reader will notice is a lack of quantification in the analysis chapters. There are two reasons for this. First, as discussed in each chapter, the positions held by individuals were often not exclusive, which in turn means that if numbers were presented, they may give a skewed view of the different positions. Additionally, while quantitative support can be helpful for establishing a position's ascendency, we were much more interested in establishing qualitative bases for discussion, rather than simply presenting a quantitative argument.

Though we have generally eschewed using numbers, it is worth noting that the lenses developed across the next three chapters rely on the more than two hundred interviews conducted. Thus, though some positions were perhaps more quantitatively well-supported, there were few positions that had single adherents, and certainly those were not used to develop the lenses in the following chapters.

CONCLUSION

Overall, again, it is key to think about these cross-cutting analyses not as particularly focused on providing definitive answers to how individuals or groups see the legalization debate, but as another set of perspectives that inform the legalization debate. Although we do not focus on numbers, we rely on the quality of the evidence, particularly within the quotes we choose to use, to convince the reader that these are valid interpretations. Even if there is disagreement, we hope that this too stirs further conversation and analysis of the legalization debate as a whole.

Chapter Nine

Contested Knowledge

How do people know what to think about marijuana legalization? Is the media responsible for our opinions? If so, how do people develop differing opinions? Questions like these are essential for understanding the legalization discourse. However, although excellent work has been done in these areas,[1] the underlying structure that provides the basis for a person's evaluation of knowledge is lacking in our understanding of the legalization debate. Thus, what makes one person "for" legalization (medical or otherwise) and one "against" is not solely the question in which we should be interested. Rather, it is important to understand the underlying knowledge constructs for opinions about marijuana legalization, and these can crosscut the categories of pro- and anti-legalization.

Therefore, although it was clear that many participants generally could be placed into the categories of "for" or "against" legalization—particularly when pressed for an answer—many of them held positions that were substantially more nuanced than a simple pro or con regarding the legalization of marijuana. Additionally, although examining the positions of different groups from teachers to law enforcement officers is essential to understanding the legalization debate, in part what it lacks is an explanation of *how* these individuals come to their positions. Though any attempt to examine that question fully is fraught, this chapter and the following two chapters examine parts of that question by looking across groups to see how individuals framed different issues important to their understanding of the legalization debate. Moreover, because no one develops opinions in a vacuum, we try in these chapters to relate these framing issues to larger issues in society.

Chapter 9 examines specifically the question of how respondents see the ideas of knowledge and expertise within the legalization debate. How individuals see these social constructs, or at least how they discuss them, is intimately linked with how they see the legalization debate moving forward. It is also essential to understand what kinds of information and expertise are admissible to individuals, as these strongly affect whether, how, and how completely an individual believes marijuana should be legalized. As such, this chapter and the next two link participant beliefs about the legalization debate to wider trends within society, taking seriously C. Wright Mills's call to link biography to history in the context of social structure.[2]

In this discussion, we hope that these characteristics help readers understand not only how groups are dealing with the legalization debate, but some of the key elements within the debate that have become important across groups. This, in turn, may help to anticipate future conversations about the legalization of what have historically been considered "vices," like prostitution or gambling.[3] If nothing else, the findings in this chapter should drive interesting discussions.

KNOWLEDGE WITHIN SOCIETY

How knowledge is constituted within society is a contested question.[4] Perhaps even more so when the knowledge in question touches directly on issues of politics or crime.[5] The question of whether or not to legalize marijuana touches both, making it a particularly interesting area to explore questions of knowledge formation, what information people use to formulate their opinions on marijuana, and what types of information they value in forming these opinions.

Given that the development of knowledge is a political topic—after all, all definitions are arguments[6]—it is appropriate to examine some of the literature on the subject of knowledge in modern society. One frame of reference that is helpful in understanding the modern constitution of knowledge is Ulrich Beck's *Risk Society*,[7] in which he examines part of the contestation that we see in the debate regarding marijuana legalization. Specifically, he explores the role of expertise and the changing constellations of knowledge creation in late modernity—a time in Western society characterized by important technological reliance on science but increasing mistrust of scientists and the scientific method.[8]

Beck and Giddens,[9] who make a similar claim, believe that the role of experts—and particularly scientists—is declining in society while reliance on complicated scientific concepts and tools is becoming increasingly important. This has significant implications regarding how people see and accept different conceptions of knowledge. Specifically, there are those who hold to the modernist framework in which scientists tend to be held in a kind of intellectual awe, with their findings considered, if not irrefutable, certainly of greater significance than experiential knowledge. Others, however—and perhaps a growing part of society as we move further into late modernity[10]—have come to view science as fallible and scientists as part of a larger system that may fail in both its findings as well as its methods of knowledge creation.

Beck and Giddens both argue that this debate about the roles of knowledge and expertise has, in part, reframed how society operates. Specifically, they argue that risk has become the central organizational principle within Western society during late modernity, with different groups essentially attempting to negotiate risk among a variety of factors, many of which are beyond their control. This, in turn, leads to existential anxiety. Other authors, notably Jock Young,[11] have examined this anxiety in relation to elements like social identity and subcultural insularity.

These ideas about how knowledge has become more contested are apparent in the development of individual positions regarding the marijuana legalization debate. Notably, individuals have different criteria in terms of what constitutes, for them, acceptable sources of knowledge. These are often associated either with specific figures of expertise—notably doctors or scientists—or with individual experiential knowledge. In both cases, these ideas are reflective of a type of risk negotiation implied by Giddens and Beck. As is discussed more completely at the end of this chapter, individuals tended to disagree on risks in terms of their framing—either risks *from* marijuana, which were often characterized by a lack of official knowledge, or risks from *not* legalizing marijuana, which tended to focus around social issues related to legalization or the individual risk for things like pain from not taking the drug.

FINDINGS

Examining the interview data regarding how individuals viewed marijuana legalization yielded interesting findings about their conceptualizations of knowledge and expertise. Notably, those interviewed broke down largely into two groups, though some individuals expressed sentiments from both. The knowledge issues focused on what kinds of information were credible and what types of expertise are acceptable upon which to base opinions regarding legalization.

Table 9.1.   Types of Credible Information and Expertise

Types	Credible Information	Expertise
1	Historical	Experiential
2	Scientific	Experimental

Knowledge

Examining the question of knowledge, we encountered individuals who believed that the science was settled regarding marijuana, as well as those who believed that many issues surrounding marijuana use were open scientific questions. For instance, one of the participants interviewed suggested that "marijuana should be legal for medical reasons: it has been used for centuries by people all over the world." The suggestion here is that society collectively *knows* the effects of marijuana already because people have been using it for a long time. This in turn suggests that the underlying structure of the knowledge is both *historical* and *experiential* in nature. We "know" about marijuana because people's use of the drug extends back centuries.

Additional examples of this approach abound. For instance, one marijuana rights group advocate stated, "so for a vast majority of human history . . . cannabis has been legal at least in some form, utilized widely in many cases, so let's get out of this little box of 1970 to 2017 and realize this has been around forever." Another advocate stated, "this plant has been in use since like 3,000 BC in China and was cited over history as one of the most effective treatments for a number of the most devastating illnesses of our time, not just in Asia, but other places in the world as well."

This view of marijuana, in turn, is contrasted with individuals who believe that the questions are still open. For instance, one respondent said, "If I were sick, I would only use it if there is proof that it worked. Right now there is no proof." This suggests, in opposition to the previous examples, that the underlying structure of the knowledge regarding marijuana is *scientific* and *experimental* in nature.

Examples of both approaches occurred frequently, though they were not always as obvious as those in the previous quotations. One less-clear instance of the historical/experiential basis of knowledge can be seen in the response of a participant who said, "I would say that it's [dosage limits for medical marijuana] more an individual basis. I mean, how do you know what dose works for me versus the other guy?" Though this seems less obvious than the first example, it still relies on the same assumptions. The respondent clearly thinks that medical marijuana has a benefit, which is implicit in the response, and the question regarding the role of doctors in determining the dosage was in response to their positive view of medicinal marijuana. This has been already decided and is not subject to further analysis. The experiential element is also implicit, suggesting that the dosage should be controlled by individuals *because they best know their use and desired effects*.

A second example of the scientific/experimental basis of knowledge can be seen in the context of the statement by a participant focused on her knowledge of marijuana as a medicine. She said, "I am not sure if it has medical benefits because I'm not a doctor." This again implies that the knowledge underlying the idea of marijuana use is scientific in orientation (only scientists know if it's useful as medicine) and experimental, which is implied in this case by the necessity of a scientific approach for its utility.

Although much of this knowledge structure was focused on the use of medical marijuana, it could also be seen in statements from participants who were speaking of adult use, or recreational marijuana use. For instance, one participant speaking of recreational use stated, "Marijuana is not a gateway drug. No proof that it is. People who use pot won't turn to heroin. Lots of people use marijuana and never use anything else. Prescription drugs are more of a gateway drug than marijuana."

This again suggests that evidence for marijuana's safety—and implicitly for the desirability of its legalization—is to be found in the common knowledge historical record. Moreover, that evidence is experientially based: society has dealt with marijuana, and therefore we already know the effects.

The relationship between the historical/experiential knowledge base and proponents of legalization was not universal, however. Several individuals used this as a basis for opposing the drug, though often this was based on personal history rather than aggregate historical experience, as in many of the examples of the historical position (e.g., "people all over the world"). For instance, one participant stated, "From my experience, it just seems like young brains shouldn't be exposed to marijuana, alcohol, or any other drugs." This, though generally opposed to legalization, relies on the experience of the respondent as the basis for knowledge rather than any kind of scientific elements.

Although there were individuals who relied on the historical/experiential knowledge base for their support for legalization, many individuals did not support legalization. Many of the respondents relied on their perceptions of the scientific evidence to support their positions regarding legalization. One respondent, not a scientist or doctor, suggested "there are medical benefits to [using marijuana] . . . for anxiety and pain." The statement that there is evidence of medical effectiveness demonstrates that many of the respondents were convinced of the veracity of the claims regarding marijuana—mostly those relating to medical use but also to the relative harm of using marijuana versus using alcohol use. Another example came from one of the marijuana business owners, who stated,

> there is a plant here that not only works [inaudible] in our system, but we don't have any sort of weird interactions with it. Our bodies are actually like accepting of this plant in our bodies. Everyone is always talking about the cure for cancer. Well, we have a plant that can reverse the growth of cancer cells and cause cancer cell death. That is a cure for cancer. It may not cure all cancers, but it cures enough. We've got kids who suddenly are not having seizures anymore and who are actually leading healthy lifestyles. I mean seizures are very debilitating, but they also cause a tremendous amount of brain trauma. Even rheumatoid arthritis—people who can't move are suddenly able to use their hands again. I mean, this is crazy . . . that people can't have this access and access to this plant.

Perhaps most interestingly, the same respondent not only talked about the supposed scientific knowledge involved in the medical uses of marijuana, but also spoke to personal use as a motivating factor contributing to the *scientific* knowledge we have about marijuana. She stated,

> I started actually . . . really thinking about what healing and health looked like from a different perspective altogether, and I was using our product on myself, just to kind of see what the . . . impact would be on different things that were going on, you know, pain, sprains, all kinds of stuff.

Thus, she believes that although scientific evidence exists for medical uses, she also believes that her own personal "experimentation" with marijuana gives a credible sense that it is effective for specific medical uses. This also demonstrates that although the experiential/experimental knowledge functioned as a dichotomy, they are not truly oppositional, as a person can hold both views simultaneously.

Although this echoes some of the literature on marijuana,[12] it is to this question—whether or not there is finality in the debate regarding the effects of marijuana—that we now turn in this analysis.

Room for Debate?

One of the dividing lines between knowledge and expertise within the debate regarding legalization is whether questions remain regarding marijuana's safety. This, though largely following the lines of the historical/experiential versus scientific/experimental view, has several unique characteristics, making it a particularly useful area to examine how individuals conceive of knowledge and expertise within the legalization debate.

Broadly speaking, there are two positions our participants took regarding the evidence of the use of marijuana's effects. The first position was taken by individuals who believed that the evidence *was* settled, that we know the effects of marijuana and that we should legislate accordingly. The second position was taken by individuals who believed that significant questions still remain regarding the effects of marijuana. For example, one of the educators who was interviewed stated, "research needs to be done to figure out dosage and stuff," though the respondent added that "then it should be legalized."

Although there was some overlap in terms of the positions taken by respondents regarding the abovementioned evidence and their positions on legalization, it's important to recognize that individuals on all sides of the legalization debate held both positions on the openness of the effects of legalization, meaning that many legalization advocates acknowledged that questions remained regarding the effects of marijuana use and the implementation of any legalization scheme. On the other hand, many individuals who were opposed to legalization (medical and adult use), felt that the evidence regarding the effects of legalization—both on individuals and society—were settled.

Interestingly, some of those who were interviewed had significant issues with the research that was being done, and thus the scientific knowledge we had was not accurate even though scientific evidence itself was considered credible. For instance, one respondent (a marijuana business owner) stated

> why would you use . . . the absolute worst product available . . . for your medical science, for your medical research, for your scientific research instead of the best products available? Because I think that what's going to happen is, even in these studies that are being conducted, the efficacy and impact are severely affected by the quality of the product that's being grown. And the quality of the product that's being grown is abysmal at the federal level compared to what's readily available from a thousand sources . . . in the state of Colorado, or Oregon, or California, or anyplace else where there's a legal system in place.

Thus, even those individuals who wished to rely (at least in part) on scientific evidence see the issue as unresolved due to the quality of the studies that have been carried out. On the other hand, those who relied more on experiential evidence tended to believe that the matter was settled. For example, one of the law enforcement officers stated, "the problem is that kids use it and then they are screwed up for the rest of their lives," and a teacher explained that "kids won't succeed in the future. Marijuana affects young people's minds permanently." Both of these were predicated on their experience rather than on particular evidence established through either scientific or medical experimentation.

Some of the respondents were quite clear in terms of where their knowledge came from. For instance, one person (a medical user) said, "I take in my personal accounts . . . my own personal [use]" as the primary source of his knowledge. In response to the statement, "it seems like the thing that informs your view most is in your personal experience with cannabis" from one of the authors, one marijuana policy advocate stated, "Absolutely. Yup." It should be added that in the cases of both of those respondents, they also cited scientific studies but made it clear that they believed their use was essential in terms of how they understood the risks (or lack thereof) of marijuana use.

This, of course, was not only true of those who used the experiential knowledge base. One anti-legalization advocate stated, "you look at the National Academy of Science reports that just came out, you look at the World Health Organization report on marijuana that came out late last year, I mean, on and on and on about objective folks looking at what's going on. It's a very grim picture, actually."

He also cited current social experience, in particular the implementation of recreational use marijuana in Colorado, as a significant source of information for his opinion. Needless to say, he viewed legalization's impacts as largely negative saying, "I'm looking at what's going on in Colorado and other states. I think it's too early to make a final conclusion, but I think things aren't going well."

As with sources of credible evidence, there was not perfect alignment in terms of those individuals who believed the question of marijuana's safety to be settled and whether or not marijuana should be legalized. Many of those who believed the question to be settled disagreed about whether the effects of marijuana use were positive or negative. This is perhaps best exemplified by comparing the business owner quoted earlier, who believed that the evidence about marijuana's effects was inconclusive but that marijuana should be legalized, nonetheless, with the teacher who believed that the question was closed and that marijuana should be outlawed based on her personal observations.

Knowledge Typology

One of the key findings to emerge from this analysis is the ability to construct a typology of knowledge acceptance in the legalization debate.

This typology revolves around two of the dimensions identified in the previous sections: whether the question of marijuana's effects is open or

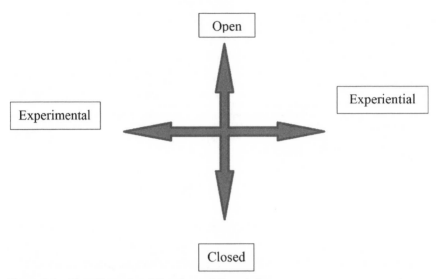

Figure 9.1.   Two-dimensional Typology of Knowledge

closed and whether experimental or experiential evidence is acceptable to answer the question. This typology represents a useful way to represent how individuals think about marijuana legalization and what evidence may be required to convince them of a particular position (see figure 9.1). Those in the top right quadrant believe that experiential evidence is primary, but the question remains open. Those in the top left believe the question remains open, but that experimental evidence is required to sufficiently answer the question. Those in the bottom left believe that the existing experimental evidence is sufficient to close the question regarding whether or not marijuana has positive effects, and those in the bottom right believe that our experiential evidence is sufficient to close the question.

Perhaps more interesting than those who clearly fall into one quadrant or another are those near the middle, who may combine evidence types to reach a conclusion or who argue for additional information. In all events, the typology can be useful in understanding where different audiences fall in relation to the question, and it offers an opportunity for thinking about how to address different kinds of knowledge concerns among proponents and opponents of legalization.

One last interesting element is that the typology could be duplicated for pro- and anti-legalization positions, since no particular quadrant seemed to have an abundance, meaning that those for and against legalization were evenly distributed across the four groupings. The same could be said for medical use versus adult recreational use of marijuana, as there were multiple positions on the question of effects and the type of evidence in both cases.

MAKING SENSE OF THE NOISE

The above gives an interesting and complicated picture in which opinions about marijuana legalization tend to revolve around issues of knowledge. However, because the context of the interviews was simply marijuana legalization—though many respondents associated marijuana legalization with drugs more generally—the above does not present a context that explains why and how individuals end up conceptualizing and valuing knowledge regarding marijuana differently. One perspective that can help make sense of this development, and indeed helps us understand how individuals discuss legalization, is the approach taken by Jock Young[13] regarding the development of identity in the context of the "exclusive society."

Essentially, Young[14] argues that society has shifted from a modern paradigm to a late modern paradigm. While this paradigm shift has two primary components, identity and economics, in both cases the change in paradigm increases inequality, since those who are excluded from the economic sphere are often cast as "other" in the social sphere. However, as "late modern" suggests, we have not left behind many of our ideas regarding identity stemming from the modern age. One way to interpret the differences regarding how individuals spoke about marijuana legalization is to think of the group that relied on scientific knowledge and experts to give credence to their fears about marijuana as those who are maintaining the modernist perspective of the role of society (as the great social integrator of deviants or "others") and the other group that relied on historical-experiential criteria for their lack of fear as those who have embraced the late modern perspective, which values diversity and inclusion.

This can be seen in some of the debate that happens regarding the historical elements of marijuana use and effects. Whereas many of those who support legalization maintain that our society has long exposure to marijuana with few ill individual effects and highlight the social costs of outlawing marijuana, those who believe in continued prohibition tend to argue that the social costs are unknown (but assumed) specifically *because* we have made marijuana illegal in the past.

For instance, one of the marijuana policy advocates suggested that because marijuana has not been legalized as alcohol and tobacco has, that's an argument for continuing the prohibition. He said,

> Alcohol has been in our history, used by a majority of the West, by a majority of Americans for five thousand years. If the majority of people regularly use marijuana—and I'm not talking in college or while they're a high school student or in their lifetime—but if they regularly, on a weekly, monthly basis, like alcohol, well, obviously then we'd have to figure something else out, another kind of policy, but the reality is there are . . . six times as many drinkers than there are people who use marijuana. There's a reason why we think of marijuana as a counterculture. And what does the word counterculture mean? It's not a part of mainstream culture, and so I think we should prevent it from being part of the mainstream culture.

This is indicative of the position mentioned earlier, that marijuana should continue to be outlawed because of the unknown social consequences due to the fact that it is outlawed. In fairness, this respondent believes that there is sufficient scientific information to infer that marijuana is (on the whole) harmful, but he also believes that the question regarding legalization is closed specifically because we already have the solution—prohibition.

On the other hand, a marijuana policy advocate with a different perspective had this to say:

> You know, this plant has been in use since like 3,000 BC in China and was cited [throughout] history as one of the most effective treatments for a number of the disease classes of our time, not just in Asia, but in other places in the world as well. Why we chose to demonize it is an issue of politics and and really good lobbying and maybe a little xenophobia.

A "marijuana rights group" advocate argued, "who are we as human beings to basically . . . outlaw something that's kinda been in our sphere for so long? And think of it this way: how can you outlaw like that when you are it? We *are* cannabis [referring to the endocannabinoid system]."

This again affects the conceptualization of knowledge regarding the use of marijuana and therefore ill effects, since those individuals not only are approaching issues of credibility differently (as mentioned earlier) but also are potentially operating within entirely different paradigms regarding society as a whole and therefore the role of drugs in it.

This, in turn, fits well with the differential perspectives offered by Young.[15] He separates recent history into two periods based on the movement from modernity into late modernity. The modernist view of deviance is one involving assimilation—moving the deviant into the mainstream. Thus, among other things, drug users (as a particular kind of deviant) are seen as either needing to be "cured" of their addiction or "punished" in order to (re)assimilate into broader society. Marijuana users are no different, at least in this regard, from other deviants or drug users.

This, too, is contested by those who take a late modern perspective. This tends to be much more individualist and identity based than the modernist perspective. Thus, marijuana use can be seen as one of many expressions of identity. Moreover, those who are shaped by the late modern perspective tend to see individual choice and self-actualization as core principles (as opposed to assimilation in the modern era), thus certain forms of deviance, like marijuana use, fit into those processes and choices more easily than in the modernist perspective.[16]

Although we did not gather age data on the respondents, there was (anecdotally) a relationship between age and support for marijuana use. This can be related to Young's[17] ideas presented earlier. In addition, these two cultural perspectives pertaining to identity and economics are at odds with one another, which can be seen in the knowledge construction typology presented earlier.

BRINGING IT BACK TO RISK

As mentioned at the outset of this chapter, in many ways the legalization debate—at least in terms of how it relates to knowledge and expertise—can be framed as a question of risk negotiation. Some individuals, often those of the modernist perspective, believe that the risk of legalizing marijuana on a large scale entails unknown consequences, which they *know* to be negative within society. Alternatively, a modernist also could argue that we *know* the risks from the science and medical research that has been done regarding the effects of marijuana, but those risks are unacceptable on a large scale.

On the other hand, an individual who has embraced a late modern perspective may suggest that we already *know* the consequences of the introduction of wide-scale marijuana use in society because we, collectively, have been using marijuana throughout much of history without significant negative consequences. Or, alternatively, that the scientific research we have done that demonstrates risk is insufficient due to the assumption of the negative impacts of marijuana use or even due to the quality of the marijuana being used.

Ultimately, then, both perspectives rely on what we could consider *contested knowledge*.[18] Even the question of what remains open to debate does not have a clear answer, as individuals from both sides of the legalization argument may adopt knowledge constructions that close the question. Moreover, those involved do not agree on the risks that should be examined, with some arguing that the health risks are primary, others the developmental risks to children, and still others countering that the societal risks in terms of maintaining prohibition (e.g., mass incarceration) are primary.

Given the fact that the sources of knowledge are contested, the openness of the question is contested, and even the worldviews of the individuals involved in the debate are largely disparate, it is unclear whether the question of legalization is fully resolvable. However, it is possible to identify a group of individuals from both sides of the debate who is willing to acknowledge the openness of the question and who can agree on acceptable sources of information. Thus, for those wishing to influence the debate moving into the future, these are the individuals on whom they should focus their efforts.

CONCLUSION

This chapter examined the role of knowledge and expertise in the marijuana legalization debate while relating it to larger changes and questions within society. As expected, when examining responses across groups, many of the participants expressed nuanced views of marijuana legalization. However, from their responses, it is possible to glean how participants viewed the questions surrounding legalization and what sources of knowledge were acceptable to them. From these, a knowledge typology consisting of how open the question of legalization was and what types of knowledge could be considered authoritative was constructed, and some implications regarding how people could be influenced were drawn.

Largely, what this analysis suggests is that legalization is likely to remain contested as long as individuals from the modernist and late modern perspectives continue to exist in society together. These different frames of reference give shape to how respondents perceive knowledge and what kinds of solutions are acceptable. In the next chapter, we turn to how respondents spoke about marijuana, particularly the kinds of metaphors they used. These, too, as we will see, are contested.

Chapter Ten

Contested Language

Though there are significant differences among respondents in terms of the types of knowledge and authority they find credible, another significant area of interest was the language they used to describe marijuana. Generally, this language was focused around specific metaphors for marijuana, and the types of metaphors that respondents used shed light on their positions regarding legalization. However, even when respondents used specific metaphors for marijuana, they were often contested: different groups used different metaphors when talking about marijuana, particularly regarding how to view the other objects in the metaphor. One example, "marijuana is like other drugs, so we should treat it that way," demonstrates how respondents can disagree either about the metaphor itself—with some saying it is *not* like other drugs—or elements within the metaphor, in that some believe our current policy regarding drugs other than marijuana is ineffective. This contestation, regarding the language we use to talk about marijuana in relation to other things, is a key part of understanding the discussion surrounding legalization.

Marijuana itself is a regularly contested part of the political landscape, and there has been no shortage of comparisons between marijuana and other products or objects. These comparisons, in turn, provide insight into both individual and collective conceptions of marijuana as both an object as well as a cultural element. Linguistics, like that by George Lakoff,[1] allows us to examine metaphors for understanding of categories of objects—what things are "like" one another and what kind of properties they share. Communication studies, specifically rhetoric, allow us to generalize in terms of how metaphors are used to create a certain image or approach in those who are receptive to specific metaphors. Thus, this chapter uses both communications and linguistics as tools to help understand how respondents talk about marijuana using metaphor and linguistic analyses.

In short, this chapter explores the use of language in regard to marijuana legalization. In so doing, it attempts to help characterize what marijuana can be compared to and to help illuminate what kinds of characteristics of marijuana are important to respondents. Additionally, through this exploration we can learn more about how other historic "vices" are seen, as well.

COMMUNICATION AND METAPHOR

"Changing culture is a matter of changing language."[2] There is a strong linguistic tie between who we are and what we do and the language we use to identify those aspects of self.[3] Additionally, though we often study language to understand how people view themselves or the world around them, people are also affected by that language. Perceptions can be changed or challenged by the language we use; however, language itself also *forms* our perceptions—we cannot understand the world without it.

The language we use, in short, provides us a way of understanding the world.[4] It encapsulates our emotions, biases, and prejudices, and it can be used to provoke emotions.[5] Metaphors are one of the principle ways that people communicate. With references going back to Aristotle,[6] the principle of something being "like" something else is fundamental to how we understand the world around us.

What this also means, however, is that metaphors are often contested. This happens for a variety of reasons, but one of the principle reasons is because through controlling which metaphor applies (or, as will be seen later, controlling how an agreed-upon metaphor is received), an individual can posit that a particular frame of reference is the correct one in which to view a problem. For instance, by comparing marijuana to "drugs" more generally, the characteristics associated with drugs in society writ large are relied upon to emphasize marijuana's illicit nature and potential physical and social detriment. On the other hand, if marijuana is "like" medicine, then other aspects of marijuana are highlighted, such as its potential for treating a variety of ailments. In short, in order to understand

Table 10.1. Metaphorical Language

	Metaphor	Simile	Metonymy
Definition	a figure of speech in which a word or phrase literally denoting one kind of object or idea is used in place of another to suggest a likeness or analogy between them	a figure of speech comparing two unlike things that is often introduced by *like* or *as*	a figure of speech consisting of the use of the name of one thing for that of another of which it is an attribute or with which it is associated
Example	"drowning in money"	"cheeks like roses"	"lands belonging to the crown"

*All from Merriam-Webster

the legalization debate surrounding marijuana, we must understand the language used by people on all sides of the debate.

There are two primary lenses with which to view metaphor. The first of these lenses is through a cognitive linguistic perspective perhaps best characterized by the work of George Lakoff.[7] Lakoff [8] takes what he considers an *experimental realism* lens when it comes to how humans perceive categories, and this perspective helps us to understand that language, though intrinsic to human nature, is experiential in nature—that it is conditioned by both biological imperatives as well as socioenvironmental elements. What this suggests is that any time we use language—and this is perhaps most true of metaphors—we rely on the human ability to think and reason, as well as a set of shared cultural expectations and associations. Thus, when speaking of an apple, we do not limit the conversation to the characteristics of a particular apple, but also to apples generally, which in turn involves cultural elements like apple pie and so forth. This is as true of marijuana as any other linguistic element.

With this view, metaphors gain a particular power. In shaping which categories (women, fire, and dangerous things, as Lackoff wrote, for example) apply through metaphor, we can profoundly shape our understanding of both the object of the metaphor and the elements used as the metaphorical item. If, for instance, we refer to marijuana as a drug, then that not only shapes our perspective of marijuana, but it also shapes our perspective of drugs due to the nature of how we understand items together through metaphor. This bi-directional effect of metaphor makes the case of marijuana particularly interesting. As can be seen later when examining the relationship between marijuana and medicine, some elements of pharmaceuticals have become reconceptualized as problematic. Although not directly related to this discussion, it is worthwhile to consider the potential effects of these metaphors on conversations surrounding topics like drug safety, which are somewhat tangential to the topic of legalization.

The second primary lens with which to view metaphor is a rhetorical lens. In this context, rhetoric refers to the art of persuasion through discourse and is inherent in debates like that of marijuana legalization.[9] The use of metaphors in persuasive rhetoric is fundamental, and these metaphors are influential. Although there are different ways to approach the idea of metaphor within rhetoric, one helpful concept for the current study is that of the archetypical metaphor.[10]

Archetypal metaphors are metaphors with specific characteristics; namely, their popularity, immunity to change, universality to human experience (like suffering), and embodiment of human motivations.[11] These elements combine, according to Osborne, to form a fifth characteristic: their persuasive potency.

These two lenses—cognitive linguistics and rhetoric—are not competing. In fact, the way in which they work together to help formulate a discourse or debate is quite clear in regard to the question of marijuana legalization, as will become apparent. In fact, from a language-based perspective, the marijuana debate can be considered the search for an appropriate archetypal metaphor to help govern our thoughts about marijuana. In this search, we also reconceptualize several other settled categories with respondent use of metaphor like "drugs."

Although our survey participants used a wide variety of metaphors to describe marijuana, we divided them into three broad categories in this chapter. The first and perhaps most common is marijuana and alcohol, the second is marijuana and tobacco, and the third is marijuana as "drugs"—which includes both licit and illicit drugs. We also discuss some other metaphors that arose during our interviews but were not as widely used by our participants.

MARIJUANA AND ALCOHOL

Given the history of alcohol in the United States, it is unsurprising that one of the most commonly used metaphors for legalization of marijuana is alcohol. A typical example of this from the "pro" perspective comes from a college professor: "We should legalize recreational marijuana like we do alcohol. People can use it on a Friday night to relax."

Albeit a relatively short metaphor—legalize marijuana like alcohol—there is complexity to this perspective. For one, it assumes—and attempts to map onto marijuana legalization—that alcohol legalization is a positive good. It further assumes that the regulation of alcohol in society is working and that the regulation of alcohol successfully mitigates any potentially negative effects.

Another example of this comes from a law enforcement officer, who said, "I think it [marijuana laws] should resemble our alcohol laws. Users should be twenty-one and over and no driving under the influence. I also think public use (smoking) should be restricted." This again demonstrates that the participant largely views the legislative framework for alcohol as effective and suggests that it can be directly implemented for marijuana legalization as well. Again, we see this in the response from a paramedic, "Both medical and recreational marijuana should be legal. But the law should have restrictions on who can buy it and use it—like we have for alcohol. People should be twenty-one to buy it, like alcohol."

An additional element to note regarding this metaphor is the idea that although marijuana regulation should resemble alcohol regulation because of the assumed effectiveness of regulation, it also assumes some *harm* in the use of marijuana—as is the case with alcohol. This is an example of the "bleed" that happens when one category (marijuana) is mapped onto another category (alcohol). In this case, it subliminally reinforces the idea that marijuana is harmful for young people and that it can be abused like alcohol.

Some respondents took a different approach to the metaphor, however, showing that even when people share perspectives, there may not be total agreement within the metaphorical construct. For instance, although many respondents simply mapped alcohol regulation onto marijuana regulation, others went further, downplaying the risk in using marijuana as compared to alcohol. For instance, a different paramedic respondent said, "Marijuana is less harmful than alcohol and tobacco. . . . It doesn't cause cancer or liver damage or other medical harms." The respondent went on to say that the restrictions should be limited only to "what's good for the economy." Thus, in this instance, the metaphor was cast in a negative light—marijuana is "like" alcohol in that it is a regulated illegal substance (and in the case of alcohol, a formerly illegal substance) but was unalike alcohol in that marijuana is less dangerous. As another example, a second law enforcement officer said, "I have always said—and still believe—that alcohol has caused more damage and ruined more lives than marijuana ever will." This kind of debate over the elements in the alcohol/marijuana metaphor happens frequently and moves the debate to alcohol *rather* than marijuana.

One example of this is from a marijuana policy advocate, who said,

> Whenever people say, "Well, alcohol is legal," [and therefore that marijuana should be] to me that doesn't make any sense. We don't want to treat marijuana like the thing that we think is so harmful. You know, we don't want to say, "Well, alcohol is so harmful, so terrible, you know, it's been very tough for society to deal with. So, okay, let's treat marijuana like that to be consistent."

This approach is interesting because while it borrows the idea that the metaphor of alcohol is controlling—otherwise the comparison would make no sense since the respondent starts with that premise (albeit in a counterfactual sense)—the argument used attempts to contest the role of alcohol rather than focusing on marijuana. Specifically, the respondent moves from the premise that alcohol regulation is good because it works to the idea that we do not want another substance like alcohol because alcohol is bad for society.

For respondents like this, then, the conversation is upended. Rather than focusing on marijuana, the conversation shifts to alcohol and its negative effects, which are then applied retroactively to the metaphor of marijuana and alcohol. In effect, the metaphor is that marijuana is like alcohol, but rather than providing a positive, applicable framework, the negative effects of alcohol on society are mapped onto marijuana.

This perspective was not limited to policy advocates. An educator said

> It's [marijuana is] like alcohol. Too much alcohol isn't good for a person and lots of people do stupid things when they are drunk. Even a drink or two

every day over a long time is not healthy. But it is legal anyway. . . . It's harmful but the state lets people use it. . . . So I guess if we use that logic, marijuana should be legal. But I still don't think it should be.

Here again we see the same basic language as that of the policy advocate. Alcohol, while still providing an apt metaphor, is recast in a negative light.

When examining the marijuana/alcohol metaphor, at issue is whether alcohol is an apt metaphor for marijuana and whether alcohol and its regulation is effective and beneficial. This is interesting because it shows how the object of the metaphor—alcohol—actually dictates the conversation, rather than marijuana itself. Alcohol has a particularly contested history in the United States, and this cultural discussion has implications for how the metaphor of alcohol is viewed.

In the next section, we examine the tobacco metaphor, which is largely used in conjunction with the alcohol metaphor but it is less, though not entirely uncontested, due to Americans' near-universal negative perceptions of tobacco.[12] However, how we view marijuana is in part shaped by the tobacco discourse, similar to the ways in which it is shaped by alcohol.

TOBACCO AND MARIJUANA

Tobacco is a metaphor used nearly as regularly for marijuana as alcohol is. In fact, tobacco and alcohol often are used in conjunction in comparisons to marijuana. There are some significant distinctions, however, between how the metaphors of alcohol and tobacco are applied to marijuana. Specifically, whereas alcohol regulation is often viewed as a model for marijuana, as seen in the previous section, tobacco is seen as an appropriate regulatory model much less often.

This seems to be largely because tobacco has become associated with specific, significant negative health outcomes in the public imagination, unlike alcohol (though alcohol, is, of course associated with some). This leads respondents to associate it with negative health consequences, and these can then be applied to marijuana through the metaphor. For example, one educator said, "We are against smoking tobacco. Why [are we] not against smoking pot? . . . Any time you put smoke in your lungs it will affect the body. . . . They [tobacco and marijuana] are both putting smoke into the lungs."

In fact, those who advocate for legalized marijuana reject the metaphor of tobacco. It was one of the few metaphors that was actively resisted. For example, one marijuana policy advocate stated, "Tobacco is vastly more damaging [than marijuana]." One marijuana industry representative said, "Tobacco has no health benefits and causes greater harm to the body [than marijuana], whereas cannabis has many, many potential health benefits and very few negative side effects." Both of these statements pointed to the *differences* between tobacco and marijuana and were being used to argue against changing the existing regulatory framework around marijuana.

Whereas policy advocates often resisted the metaphor of tobacco, other respondents felt that, like alcohol, tobacco regulation provided a general analogue for marijuana regulation. For instance, one paramedic respondent stated, "The law to legalize marijuana should be the same as tobacco: [Someone] must be eighteen to purchase recreational [marijuana]. Farmers should grow [marijuana] and sell to help the U.S. agricultural system." In an interesting example, another respondent used the metaphor of the tobacco industry as a reason to argue against legalization, stating:

> I think that legalization has become about one thing, and that thing is money. Making a small number of people rich, just like we had for tobacco—the tobacco industry. And, you know, making a small number of people rich because, really, in these types of addictive, habit-forming businesses, you don't make money from occasional users.

In these comments, the respondents directly map the domains of tobacco—including the industry and regulation—onto the nascent marijuana industry and the associated regulation. Similar to the argument regarding alcohol, when coupled with the resistance to the tobacco metaphor, the argument over legalization moves to whether or not *tobacco* is adequately regulated and what its effects on society are. However, unlike the alcohol discourse, most agree that tobacco regulation has not been successful (see groups like the *Truth* campaign and the lawsuits against tobacco companies, for example), though cases in which respondents referenced both alcohol *and* tobacco tend to support a similar regulatory framework. However, as will be seen in the following section, this is largely because when alcohol and tobacco are associated together, they become part of the larger domain of "drugs."

MARIJUANA AND "DRUGS"

The situation becomes more complex when it comes to the metaphor of marijuana as a "drug." This is because marijuana *is* a drug, so rather than metaphor, we are using metonymy. This distinction—comparing one thing to another (metaphor and simile) and replacing one of the items in the comparison with a closely related idea (e.g., "that guy is a real suit")—follows the same pattern. In both cases, we map one domain (all the things we associate with drugs) onto another (marijuana). In the case of our respondents, often this meant putting together alcohol, tobacco, and marijuana into the category of drugs (oftentimes "other drugs").

Respondents used the term "drugs" in two ways, however. The first is mentioned above: referring to other psychoactive substances like alcohol and tobacco. The other is in reference to pharmaceuticals. In both instances, the undergirding idea is that marijuana is "like" these other substances—either psychoactive substances (both licit and illicit) or pharmaceuticals.

For example, in the frame of psychoactive substances, one paramedic respondent indicated that

> Marijuana should be legalized. If people want to use it to relax, they should be allowed to do it. It doesn't cause cancer or liver damage or other medical harms. If the other drugs [alcohol and tobacco] are legal, then marijuana should be, too."

This is a somewhat normative case. Drugs are considered to be harmful—like tobacco and alcohol—and because marijuana fits into that category but is *less* harmful, it should be regulated like the others, in this case, tobacco and alcohol. This type of metonymy, however, can cut both ways, rhetorically speaking. For instance, one marijuana policy advocate stated, "Well, I think . . . people are prone to marijuana addiction like they are to other drug [marijuana and alcohol] addiction." One educator added, "Why are we encouraging smoking another drug?"

An additional element is added when the drugs referenced in the metonymy are illegal. For example, one homemaker said, "[Marijuana] is a
gateway. People use it and then want to use more drugs. They start with
other drugs and then go to harder drugs."

The argument shifts from specific elements of marijuana legalization
to the metaphorical element of "drug" effects. This was not just the case
for psychoactive substances, however, it was also the case for pharmaceuticals. One lawyer respondent, for instance, said, "Patients shouldn't
be allowed to use as much [marijuana] as they want legally. It should be
more controlled, like other prescription drugs." In a similar context, one
senior citizen argued, "[Marijuana] makes people use other drugs. Once
you get used to being high, then you want to try other highs and you can't
stop. Once you start using too many drugs it's too hard to stop."

These references to "drugs" in the larger sense—and perhaps especially
when it comes to illicit drugs—rely on preconceived cultural ideas of
what drugs "do" and what they are. Addiction is arguable when it comes
to marijuana, but applying the standard of "drugs" to marijuana specifically means that we adopt the *idea* of addiction into the specific case of
marijuana.

This, again, can cut both ways, however. One student respondent said,
"I support the legalization of marijuana because it is no worse than any
other drugs that people use. Some drugs that are prescribed by doctors
have serious medical side effects, some of which can last a long time or
be permanent." In this case, other drugs are *worse* than marijuana, so its
legalization is recognition of the lesser harm. This is, however, predicated
on the idea that marijuana is *like* other drugs in other respects—that it has
effects that are in some ways similar to other drugs. This is evident in a
statement from a marijuana scientist who stated,

> If we just take the existing procedures for policy and regulation that we have
> for any other drug and apply it to cannabis as a potential novel therapeutic, a
> lot of the concerns there [treating cannabis as different than other drugs] go
> away. . . . Recognizing that with any other medication we have on the mar-
> ket, there are risks and benefits and not everybody responds the same way.

In this example, the respondent makes the explicit argument that marijuana is *like* the other pharmaceuticals and argues directly for a specific
regulatory regime to be applied on that basis.

It is worth noting that there was a subset of respondents who did not use the drug metaphor (or metonymy) but who instead referenced "medicine." For instance, one of the marijuana policy advocates stated, "Wait a second! This [marijuana], this is medicine! It's not just a recreational drug, it's beyond all that." He later referred to marijuana with high THC content as "strong medicine." Another advocate stated, "We shouldn't tax medicine [referring to marijuana]. Period."

The distinction between "medicine" and "drugs" is interesting, specifically because of the imprecise nature of the latter term. Drugs can be either illicit or licit, whereas references to medicine nearly always refer to licit substances. Further still, medicine is arguably much more positive in connotation than even "pharmaceuticals," which (particularly today) have been tainted by addiction and over-prescription.[13]

Interestingly, however, this too was contested. One policy advocate, for instance, argued

> I think we should treat marijuana like any other medicine in that it should be subject to those rigorous tests and we should figure out which parts make sense to prescribe and so make that sharp distinction [between recreational and medical use] that, unfortunately, the ways these laws are written in most places, we're taking about a distinction that's very . . . blurry.

The distinction he draws here is actually between "medicine" and "drugs" (i.e., drugs used for recreation). This is the very distinction that causes people to use the term "medicine," but as the previous quote shows, that terminology can also be contested.

In short, "drugs" as a referent for marijuana has many of the same characteristics as alcohol does. However, given the difficulty of pinning down a precise meaning for drugs in the sense used by respondents, it creates additional space for debate, though this tends to revolve around the regulatory process associated with the drugs or medicine rather than the legalization of marijuana. As such, it represents one of the clearest examples of metaphor and metonymy for marijuana and provides ample examples of why legalization remains contested.

OTHER METAPHORS

Though alcohol, tobacco, and "drugs" represent the most common meta-phors/metonyms used by our respondents in conjunction with marijuana, they were not the only metaphors used. In some ways, the lack of wide-spread use of the following metaphors highlights the debate surrounding the appropriate way to view marijuana and its legalization. The objects of the metaphors in the "other metaphor" category tend to be less contested than tobacco, alcohol, or drugs, so using any of these metaphors represents moving marijuana into less combative territory.

One of the most direct metaphors was that marijuana should "be legal like a tomato." This is a particularly good metaphor. A tomato, like mari-juana, is grown, and it can be consumed, but it is also largely viewed as having no harmful effects on society. If this was the archetypal metaphor, a concept discussed more in the conclusion, the argument over marijuana legalization would probably end, as there would be little need to regulate something like a tomato.

Not all of the other metaphors were this clear, however. One respon-dent, in particular, offered a series of potential metaphors for marijuana: "We could talk about it like coffee. We could talk about it like sugar. . . . We could talk about it like Five-Hour Energies [the supplement] or Red Bull. We could talk about it like caffeine pills. . . . I mean, it's all drugs." All of these examples of metaphor are interesting for the same reasons (except drugs). It is clear from the response that the respondent is pro legalization due to the metaphors chosen. One question to ask is why it is clear from the metaphors. The answer is because listeners immediately know what those metaphors have in common. In other words, it's easy for us to understand what elements of each domain map onto the subject of the metaphor—marijuana.

In the previous examples—particularly things like sugar and Five-Hour Energy—there is a tacit admission that marijuana *can* be harmful, but like those other items, should be legal and are harmless when taken moderately. A similar logic applies to caffeine pills. The last statement, regarding them all being "drugs" is particularly interesting, since it is an example of how metaphors apply not just from the object to the subject of the metaphor (e.g., from caffeine pills to marijuana) but also the reverse. In this case, the idea that all of those (relatively) harmless substances are "drugs" negates the usual negativity associated with the domain of drugs.

These examples provide the best evidence for the utility of persuasive metaphors for marijuana and its legalization. If someone can be convinced that a particular metaphor is more apt, then he or she may adopt those elements that are helpful to his or her side of the legalization debate. Thus, much of the legalization debate, at least in terms of the respondents for this book, takes place on the level of metaphor.

ARCHETYPAL METAPHORS
AND THE LEGALIZATION DEBATE

As can be seen in the previous examples, much of the debate regarding legalization revolves around the use of metaphors—both for the drug itself and for appropriate legalization regimes. However, as is also seen, the metaphors themselves are often contested. As such, the legalization debate can be thought of in some respects as the struggle for the archetypal metaphor—and how that metaphor will be used.

Each of the metaphors offered in this chapter—alcohol, tobacco, and drugs, notably—has particular utility for each side of the debate. Thus, much of the debate surrounds not just which of the metaphors is appropriate, but what parts of the domain of the metaphorical object should be applied. In the case of marijuana's similarities to alcohol, the debate surrounds both the negative effects of alcohol and the failures of the regulatory system on one hand versus the legality of alcohol and society's tolerance of its negative effects. This, in turn, centers the debate on alcohol rather than marijuana, and the "winner" of that debate (if ever there is one) controls our understanding—to a degree—of marijuana. The same is true for the other metaphorical objects mentioned in the previous analysis.

One interesting thing not fully explored here is the fact that mapping affects both the subject of the metaphor as well as the object. So as our cultural understanding of marijuana changes, so too will our understanding of other "drugs" or alcohol by virtue of the use of the marijuana metaphor. For if something is "like" something else, then what is true of one must affect the other.

This struggle surrounding the language we use to talk about marijuana should interest anyone involved in the legalization debate, particularly as new metaphors are introduced. Notably, some respondents pointed out the parallels between marijuana businesses and other types of businesses. As such references increase, there may be more use of the marijuana-as-business metaphor. Indeed, the idea of marijuana as "big business" did arise, particularly among those advocating complete legalization (e.g., without restrictions) as a way of averting the negative elements perceived as the result of "big business."

In addition to helping us to understand how the debate is progressing, the use of metaphors in the legalization debate may also provide a method by which we can determine which "side" of the debate seems to be gaining ground. One of the most influential books regarding the marijuana debate relies directly on the metaphor of alcohol. Called *Marijuana Is Safer, So Why Are We Driving People to Drink?*[14] the book's title (and much of its content) can be read as a method of reestablishing the negative aspects of alcohol specifically so the argument can be made that marijuana should be legal *like* alcohol is. Indeed, in the larger literature of "vice crime," marijuana use often is viewed in the same vein as sex work, which has been decriminalized (much like marijuana) in some places.

Watching the marijuana discourse develop along these lines can give insight to the debate as it is carried out across society. Understanding the metaphors can, therefore, give us the ability to better understand not only the debate, but how those engaging in the debate see cannabis and related subjects.

CONCLUSION

Although there are many elements that are important to the debate surrounding marijuana legalization, there are few that have more relevance than that of language. How the discourse regarding marijuana use and regulation develops will in large part dictate how potential policy change progresses and how those changes are implemented and accepted. Part of this discourse revolves around the metaphors we use to describe marijuana and its legalization. Regardless of the metaphor chosen—alcohol, tobacco, or something else entirely—the ability to control the archetype of how we see marijuana is key to driving the development of the discourse.

Thus, this chapter makes clear both how respondents regard marijuana and its legalization as well as how we should understand specific metaphors for marijuana. This metaphorical discussion, then, takes place on two levels: what particular metaphor applies and how we should understand the object of the metaphor. This sometimes takes the debate regarding legalization far afield about the effects *not* of marijuana itself, but rather the metaphorical objects with which we can associate with it.

One last example is worth mentioning to close the chapter. Several legalization policy advocates referred to themselves not as political operatives or policy analysts (often their official titles), but rather as "abolitionists"—referring to their desire to abolish prohibitions on marijuana use. That phrase, however, suggests a period of history of oppression that not only frames how those individuals assess our current circumstances regarding marijuana, but also how they see themselves in the scope of history.

All told, understanding the language surrounding the marijuana debate is essential to understanding the debate itself. As the discourse continues to develop and as the language continues to change, the metaphors themselves will also continue to evolve and shape that debate. Examination of the language, then, is essential in understanding how individuals and society regard the legalization debate.

Chapter Eleven

Contested Politics

"Over the previous decades marijuana has been a veritable political mine-field."[1] If recent statements and reactions to them by the current (as of this writing) attorney general Jeff Sessions are any indication, the political sensitivity of the issue of marijuana is unlikely to change in the near future. However, despite contention surrounding this subject within the political system, there has been little examination of the types of political issues people connect with marijuana and its legalization.

What little information we do have regarding general perceptions of the effects of legalization tends to focus on the criminal justice system—either helping to reduce crime by keeping marijuana illegal or by legalizing marijuana thereby reducing incarceration for drug crimes. In the following sections, these political issues are highlighted, as those competing political narratives were apparent in the respondents' statements. This is perhaps unsurprising, since cultural references to these narratives are clear in both political discourse[2] as well as popular culture.[3]

This chapter examines those primary political narratives and identifies some others that regularly came up during interviews. In many respects, this analysis involves tying together the previous two chapters on language and knowledge through the different participants' particular approaches to the topic of legalization. Overall, the political narratives—especially those involving crime and criminal justice—have dominated the discourse on legalization. However, as legalization has become more widespread, other political considerations have arisen, and the political elements of these narratives are also considered.

MARIJUANA AND CRIME

Although a significant portion of the respondents considered marijuana a special category of drug crime (particularly in the case of law enforcement and lawyers), many linked use of marijuana to crime in other ways. For instance, a law enforcement officer suggested that marijuana legalization would lead to "more crime. Not so much violent crimes, but stupid crimes [like] trespassing." Another officer agreed: "We'll have more people arrested for doing stupid things when they're high."

A third officer suggested that marijuana was linked to crime in a different way: "They will commit crimes to get money to buy it [marijuana]." One of the respondents in the legal profession had a related comment: "There may be . . . more people arrested for other [marijuana-related] crimes." Similarly, a respondent who is a judge stated: "They [marijuana users] commit crimes to get more. Then they end up committing some other crime and end up here [in court]." Even a marijuana legalization advocate allowed that "At the margins, there's a debate to consider if someone's committing crime because of dependence [on marijuana]."

All of these perspectives link marijuana directly to crime, either through its use, which causes behavioral changes, or through addiction, which causes related criminal behavior. These perspectives, in turn, align with media representations of drug users as "addicts," which often drive peoples' opinions about the development of related criminal activity or "drug-related" crimes.[4] These opinions also rely on existing discursive frames—in this case a "safety" frame (e.g., violent crime would increase as law enforcement focused on marijuana enforcement) that are regularly drawn out in legalization battles like California's Proposition 19 debate.[5]

Certainly not all respondents believed that crime would increase with marijuana legalization. Several respondents suggested that legalization would have no effect at all. A representative from the marijuana industry suggested that the effect of marijuana on crime is "none. I don't think there is any, other than the fact that it's illegal." A different law enforcement officer than those mentioned earlier suggested that "legalization probably will not affect crime rates or the calls we respond to."

However, a third perspective regarding the relationship between marijuana legalization and crime also is worth highlighting: some respondents maintain that marijuana legalization would *decrease* crime. One EMT, for instance, said, "We should legalize recreational marijuana because the crime rate would go down." Other respondents agreed with that legalization argument. For instance, one of the cannabis industry representatives said, "you can lower crime [by legalizing marijuana]. You can get rid of the violence associated with it." Though many respondents argued this perspective, others also believe it would reduce crime at the individual level. One student, for instance, said, "Legal marijuana does not lead to more crime. People who are high don't want to commit crime. They just get mellow and happy."

This trichotomy, that marijuana legalization will increase crime, that it will not affect crime, or that it will lower crime, frames a significant portion of the debate regarding legalization. Additionally, whereas the public debate tends to focus on whether crime increases or decreases, the lack of engagement in the marijuana legalization debate by many people may be in part due to their belief that legalization would not affect crime or other social phenomena. In turn, these perspectives on legalization rely on existing ideas in the discourse surrounding marijuana and other drug use—that addicts commit crime to get drugs, that people do "stupid" things when high, or that marijuana causes one to "chill" and not commit additional crimes.

MARIJUANA ENFORCEMENT *AS* SOCIAL ILL

Contradicting the supposed link between marijuana and crime, which is generally considered a social ill, many respondents suggested that enforcement of current marijuana laws was the social ill and thus legalization would solve a problem. This is in line with what is generally a newer social frame for legalization that considers the social cost of enforcement.

Perhaps most emblematic of the new frame is Michelle Alexander's book *The New Jim Crow: Mass Incarceration in an Age of Colorblindness*,[6] which posits that drug laws are a key part of the control of minorities within society through mass incarceration. Although less focused on racial elements than Alexander, many respondents seemed to share the belief that the problem was not with legalization but with continued criminal penalties for marijuana use.

For example, one marijuana advocate said, "the other aspect of not just marijuana reform, but drug policy reform, is . . . how the incarceration of people destroys families and contributes to the arrested development of them as human beings, both financially and just the way they navigate the world." Other respondents shared this perspective. Another advocate for marijuana legalization said, "I think we've got to get out of the business of incarcerating people for marijuana. You know, the overincarceration of America finds its root in marijuana. There are far too many arrests. There are 800,000 arrests every year for marijuana and for possession, as well, and that's got to stop."

Still a third advocate linked it more directly to race and incarceration, saying,

> when we have a Justice Department that just overturned the previous administration's decision on private prisons, when we're seeing an administration that is openly flaunting increased enforcement against people of color [by officers] who may or may not have a legitimate suspicion of their immigration status, you know marijuana is going to be again and again and again used as another way for people to be [jailed], to put them into this system that fundamentally opposes them.

Interestingly, it was not just legalization advocates who acknowledged the problem of incarceration. One anti-legalization policy advocate said, "I think I understand more now . . . the negative consequences—even when you don't go to prison—of an arrest or an arrest record [related to marijuana]."

However, it was not just professional advocates or industry representatives who felt this way. One of the respondents involved in the legal profession said, "The War on Drugs has become part of the prison-industrial complex. It is used to fill prisons and jails to keep those people [prison employees] employed." Others, though not linking marijuana enforcement directly to mass incarceration per se did link it to social ills. For instance, one student said, "[legalization of marijuana] would crack down on crime and clear out prisons that are overpopulated for drug-related crimes." Another student had a similar sentiment, stating, "There are too many people in jail and prison for having marijuana. Legalization would depopulate jails and decrease expenses. It's mostly illegal for political reasons anyway." One marijuana policy advocate's assessment of the harms of enforcement of marijuana laws was particularly strong: "The harms of [marijuana] prohibition are far greater than any harms that come from marijuana consumption."

This perspective—that the enforcement is worse than the social cost of legalization—is an important one for understanding the current status of the marijuana debate. Whereas earlier attempts at legalization, like Proposition 19 in California, did rely somewhat on the idea of the social costs of the War on Drugs, that frame has been refined, tying together significant social ills focused around issues of race and mass incarceration, which was clear in the statements by many of the participants.

TANGENTIAL ENFORCEMENT PROBLEMS

Though many of the respondents suggested either that crime was a direct result of marijuana use or that the mass incarceration of drug users was a significant social ill, there were other issues that arose from respondents related to marijuana and its legalization that did not necessarily fall under these headings. For instance, one respondent, a lawyer, said,

> People won't stop using [marijuana] if it remains illegal. It's like Prohibition. People wanted to drink and found ways to do it—the violence [was] associated with making it illegal. There was so much violence that we had to re-legalize it [alcohol]. Now there is little [violence]. The same pattern holds true for marijuana.

A marijuana reform advocate made a broadly similar point: "It wasn't marijuana specifically that drew me in [to the legalization debate]. It was coming to understand the whole issue of the War on Drugs and drug prohibition, particularly the violence that's associated with it." Identifying enforcement as the source of violence is not new. This was an element used in the "safety" frame by those advocating for legalization in the Proposition 19 debate, which has been regularly featured in literature advocating for marijuana legalization for some time.[7] Characterizing those against legalization as "marijuana prohibitionists" is an attempt to capitalize on these negative associations with the results of the prohibition of alcohol.

Violence, however, was not the only tangential problem identified by our respondents. Several respondents pointed toward more mundane social benefits to their positions. For instance, one law enforcement officer suggested that "we should make it [marijuana] legit and put the smugglers out of business." Another suggested that it would reduce the paperwork required of the police due to the volume of marijuana-related incidents, thus allowing police to focus on other crimes. Similarly, a lawyer said, "legalizing marijuana would free up police resources, because we wouldn't be spending time on finding pot smokers or those who are possessing."

These responses imply that one of the tangential problems of maintaining criminalization of marijuana is that police are not able to focus on "real" crime. Thus, enforcement of marijuana laws, according to this perspective, actually increases the amount of "real" crime being committed or occurring without detection.

Lest it seem as if this is not a widespread perspective, the state of Washington's recreational legalization initiative[8] enshrines this basic perspective in its very first clause: "Sec. 1. The people intend to stop treating adult marijuana use as a crime and try a new approach that: (1) Allows law enforcement resources to be focused on violent and property crimes."

Not all respondents agreed with this perspective, however. Some believed that marijuana legalization would *increase* enforcement, primarily through regulation. For example, one respondent who practices law foresees "lots of overcrowding as people are charged and have to go to court. Defense cases will go up. May lead to a lot of court overcrowding, and we may need to use other courts/diversion programs."

Additionally, several respondents brought up the difficulty of enforcement for crimes like driving under the influence (DUI) in relation to marijuana. One educator, for instance, said "there is no way to test for being high, so it's hard for the police—especially if someone is driving high." A similar perspective was shared by an EMT who said legalization "might be tricky because of the current no-smoking laws and an inability to quickly test drivers [for marijuana use]."

Thus, though not universal, the perspective that current enforcement of marijuana laws represents a problem for overall crime enforcement holds significant power. This is perhaps unsurprising given the focus on the negative effects of mass incarceration and the War on Drugs mentioned in the previous section. In any event, many respondents seemed to agree that marijuana enforcement causes tangential problems for society, either due to additional unrelated crime or through the direct creation of violence.

TAXATION AND RESOURCES

One area directly associated with politics is the taxation of (legalized) marijuana and how to distribute those resources. Of the responses from all respondents, the most frequent was that marijuana should be taxed if legal. For instance, one teacher said, "Marijuana should be taxed and the revenue used for schools. It could also be used to pay for infrastructure for the state or health care." Another educator expressed relatively similar sentiments, "It [marijuana] should be taxed and the money should go to agencies that help. Any nonprofits, for example, but especially to groups that help children with diseases or who have cancer."

Teachers were not the only respondents who felt this way. One law enforcement respondent said, "We should tax it and make money." An EMT respondent said marijuana "should be taxed and . . . it would help create jobs in the state." One paramedic respondent also stated that marijuana "should be taxed like it is in other states and the money given to the schools and also used to fix roads." Another paramedic said, "The long-term impact of legalization is the increase in tax dollars to the local government. They would make a lot of money that can be used to improve the communities."

In fact, across nearly all groups, the issue of taxation was one that was most agreed upon. Even many of those who did not believe in legalization for recreational use believed that medical marijuana should be taxed. There were even a number who did not think that marijuana should be legalized at all but who felt that *if* it was going to be legalized, it should be taxed. For example, relating marijuana to alcohol, one educator said, "Even a drink or two every day over a long time isn't healthy. But it is legal anyway. The government taxes it and we make a lot of money . . . so I guess if we use that logic, marijuana should be legal. But I still don't think it should be."

A male respondent, after stating his support for marijuana to remain illegal, said, "In the next few years, marijuana will be legal in more states and there will be pros and cons for that. The pros are that we will have more taxes funding the government; the con is that there may be more people walking around high."

A more nuanced view differentiated between medical and recreational use of marijuana. Several respondents said that medicine should not be taxed. One particularly good example of this was stated by a policy advocate who said, "You know, our PT director said it best. He's like 'look, we shouldn't tax medicine period.' And I was like, 'Alright, cool. I could sell that.' I believe that. It's easy—you shouldn't tax medicine."

What is perhaps most interesting about the issues of taxation is not the widespread agreement between respondents that marijuana, if legalized, should be taxed. It is instead the underlying assumption that there is not only a social or political cost to marijuana remaining illegal, but that there is also a financial cost. The relative boon of a marijuana tax is assumed by nearly all those who suggested uses for the money, but few mentioned increased regulatory enforcement costs or increased bureaucracy that may be required to provide an appropriate framework for taxation and regulation. For some, this may be because they were reluctant to consider the consequences of legal marijuana in general, but for many it seems that the implicit balance between the potential social costs of marijuana and the financial benefits weighed in favor of the latter.

ROLE OF CURRENT INSTITUTIONS

Throughout the conversations with respondents, one of the clear themes that arose in terms of politics was the importance of current institutions. This was represented in a variety of ways, and not all respondents viewed the current institutions positively, though nearly all respondents framed their responses to legalization in terms of the current institutional structure. For instance, one of the clearest examples dealt with medical marijuana. Many people who believed that medical marijuana should be legalized also believed that the current governmental structure—the Food and Drug Administration (FDA)—was sufficient to account for the needs of legalization.

This, in some ways, is an extension of the "marijuana as medicine" metaphor mentioned in the previous chapter. For instance, one anti-legalization advocate said,

> Well, I mean, they should test it [marijuana] like they would medicine. We should know what's in it. So yes the FDA should be determining what medicine is. I think that it [the legalization debate] is talking about medicine and getting a medical product through the FDA [which] regulates the trials is how that works and I think that should continue.

In another example of this perspective, a law enforcement officer said,

> People are not allowed to make their own aspirin or antibiotic, why should they be able to grow their own pot? It should be sold at Rite Aid or CVS [drugstores] for a true medical reason, not [for] a stubbed toe or headache. It should have to pass FDA medical tests for specific uses, for specific ailments.

For both of these respondents, the current regulatory structure for medicine is deemed adequate for marijuana. In fact, respondents cited a number of political structures but none was universally suggested, even in the case of the FDA. For example, one legalization advocate stated, "Marijuana's not a drug, it's a plant, and so what are the implications of the FDA deciding how people are able to use a plant that they can grow inside their own house?" This response is interesting, because it indicates that the current FDA is *not* adequate for the regulation of marijuana, even if the concerns revolve around intrusion into personal life. This was not the only case of inadequacy of a current political structure. One state representative from a state considering legalization said, "There will be a committee to oversee the implementation of the law. The details of the law have not yet been worked out." Another political respondent, a city manager, suggested that there was not yet infrastructure in place to monitor dispensaries if marijuana was legalized in his state, saying,

> As a city manager, I may have to regulate dispensaries if the city wants them. The city council will have to decide if they want to allow them in the city, and if they vote "yes," we will have to determine where they will be

located, how many there will be, who will own them, and how to regulate them. The law is not clear on that.

On the whole, however, most respondents felt that the current institutions would be able to handle the legalization of marijuana—medical, recreational, or both. Although most respondents were not explicit, they regularly cited the FDA as a regulatory body and drew on alcohol as an example of a taxation scheme, demonstrating that most believe our current institutions would play a primary role.

STATE, FEDERAL, OR NONE

The current state of marijuana—legal in some states but illegal at the federal level—has been called a "constitutional crisis."[9] Three different perspectives emerged from our respondents' general comments regarding marijuana legalization: that marijuana should be regulated at the federal level, the state level, or not regulated at all. It also should be noted many respondents believed that marijuana should be regulated at multiple levels.

One good example of a respondent talking about the level of regulation was from a marijuana rights group leader who said, "I think the federal government needs to retool how it looks at things. I think they got the necessity to take a real strong look at the Controlled Substances Act [CSA] and amend it so that it can comport with international law and take marijuana scheduling away from it [the CSA]." The focus in this comment was on deregulation of marijuana at the federal level. However, the same respondent also said, "Medicine has always been regulated at the state level. I see there's no reason to bring in the federal government to regulate state-based medicine. I think that it takes [the decision] closest to the patients, understanding that it's the patient that's important." Although this respondent spoke about federal regulation, it was in service to moving regulatory authority toward the states—at least in terms of medical marijuana.

Other respondents also supported primarily state-level legislation. One interesting example of this was from a cannabis industry lobbyist, who works at the federal level. He said,

So everyone's worried that the feds are going to start enforcing federal law and that's a big concern for us [the cannabis industry] and one of the things we're working on is making sure these guys in [Washington] D.C. understand its important for your state. . . . The ultimate decider should be the states themselves and the voters of that state.

One reason the previous responses are interesting is because marijuana legalization historically has been a liberal issue.[10] On the other hand, "states rights" issues tend to lean conservative, thus we see advocates for increasing states rights on a liberal issue.[11]

However, some respondents were proponents of regulation at higher levels. For instance, one anti-legalization advocate stated, "We have different penalties for all kinds of crimes depending on where you live, but the overall regulation and monitoring [of marijuana] . . . transcends the states." Another respondent said, "Legalization should be made at the national level and regulated by the government and not left up to individual states. At this rate, at least the pot industry would have the same rules and regulations across the country and be taxed the same [way]."

One particularly interesting response came from a scientist who works with marijuana and its effects. He said,

There needs to be some reconciliation of the disconnect between state and federal law. And the reason I say that is not because I think that we can't have, you know, wishy-washy mixed messages, but rather because when you look at how things are handled and the important things—doing things the right way in terms of making cannabis available and legal—some of the major issues and concerns I have are that all of the regulatory bodies that control drugs, drug manufacturing, drug labeling, quality control, and medicine, those are all federal agencies. And the states don't have the knowledge or the infrastructure to do this the right way, and that's causing problems.

This response is particularly interesting because it deals with both the ability of current institutions to regulate marijuana, which was explored in the previous section, along with the federal-state question. This was perhaps the most explicit articulation of the federal-state problem—that the current differentiation between federal law and state law regarding marijuana was untenable—but as the city manager in the previous section mentioned, the law is still being worked out.

Finally, there was a relatively small group of respondents who believed that marijuana should not be regulated at all. In some cases, this lack of regulation was related to the idea that drugs in general should not be regulated—a more libertarian perspective—but in others it was directly related specifically to marijuana as a unique drug. Illustrating the first type, one respondent said, "I just understand that drug prohibition doesn't actually work, and so bring it [use of drugs] out to the open; we can manage it better that way. That includes marijuana, obviously." One example of the second type was given by a respondent who works in marijuana policy and said,

> I would like to think that there's a general trend among the vast majority of Americans toward less intrusive governmental policies and allowing people to have a lot more control over their bodies and minds as long as they're not infringing on the rights of others. . . . And being willing to support the will of the people versus potential political backlash [for legalization] that's unique to marijuana.

ASSESSMENT

So what are we to make of the myriad perspectives of the politics of marijuana legalization represented in this chapter? First, though legalization has been a politically contested issue for more than thirty years, there are still a significant number of different perspectives regarding the correct way to handle it. Not only that, but there is reason to believe—at least among our respondents—that the current regulatory system—with the exception of medical marijuana—is inadequate to take on marijuana if it is legalized for recreational use. Moreover, although many respondents believed that states are responsible for regulating marijuana, some participants believed that regulation at the federal level was more appropriate or that the states couldn't handle marijuana regulation at all.

Outside these general institutional concerns, there was a larger social debate regarding the relative costs and benefits of the legalization of marijuana. Specifically, although many respondents felt that marijuana use contributed to crime, others believed strongly that the harms of marijuana enforcement outweighed any harms caused by consumption.

This, in many ways, has become the central debate regarding legalization, especially as the movement against mass incarceration has gained momentum. In fact, the War on Drugs and its potential failure was used by some participants to argue for the legalization of *all* drugs, rather than marijuana specifically.

In addition, many advocates for marijuana policy liberalization or legalization cited instances of social disparity in enforcement or personal negative encounters with law enforcement over marijuana possession and use as their reason for becoming interested in advocating for legalization. This area of the legalization debate is hotly contested, and it's worth noting that it intersects heavily with the previous two chapters. Those involved in the politics of marijuana legalization—which includes most of us who have an opinion about it and vote—rely on both specific sets of knowledge (e.g., either scientific or experiential) for our arguments and a set of metaphors to communicate this knowledge. Thus, much of what is contained in the politics of legalization depends largely on what underpins the narratives that each side constructs, namely those same knowledge constructs and metaphors.

Interestingly, although respondents represented different points of view across all of the issues mentioned in this chapter, there was more agreement than disagreement across political boundaries. In other words, though many have viewed marijuana legalization through the lens of partisan politics, that lens may be insufficient for understanding the current legalization debate. This is because, despite liberal elements involved in the marijuana debate, it has transcended traditional political boundaries.[12] One reason for this is because marijuana legalization advocates use "states rights" to encourage traditionally conservative populations (like law enforcement, for example), while at the same time capitalizing on the generally liberal belief in the principle of using taxes for infrastructure. This was evident in the different reasons respondents gave for supporting legalization and can be seen in the previous sections.

What this means for marijuana legalization is unclear, however. Though the politics of legalization seem to be moving away from debates about the specific harms caused by use, which characterized an earlier era of prohibition, it is by no means certain that the debate has become fixed, nor that legalization will continue unabated. Recent political circumstances have also changed, making the position of the federal government vis-à-vis state government less clear.

Whether or not these changes will affect people like our respondents remains unclear. Although this chapter demonstrates the influence of existing narratives like those surrounding the War on Drugs and the reasons people give for legalization (or keeping marijuana illegal), what is uncertain is how quickly the narratives can change and how concrete they are once they are formed. As marijuana enforcement changes, if in fact it does change, it is possible that many of the rationales people give for legalization may fall to the wayside. What is certain is that although there seems to be a growing coalition across traditional political lines, there is still a strong resistance from some to the legalization of marijuana for any use at all.

Notes

CHAPTER ONE

1. Stringer, R. J. & Maggard, S. R. (2016). "Reefer Madness to Marijuana Legalization: Media Exposure and American Attitudes toward Marijuana (1975–2012)." *Journal of Drug Issues* 46 (4): 428–45; see also Newton, D. E. (2013). *Marijuana: A Reference Handbook.* Santa Barbara, CA: ABC-CLIO.

2. Yeric, J. L. & Todd, J. R. (1989). *Public Opinion: The Visible Politics.* Itasca, IL: F. E. Peacock Publishers.

3. Marion, N. (2007). *A Primer in the Politics of Criminal Justice.* New York: Criminal Justice Press.

4. Swift, A. (2016, October 19). "Support for Legal Marijuana Use up to 60 Percent in U.S. Gallup Research." www.gallup.com/poll/196550/support-legal-marijuana.aspx.

5. Geiger, A. (2016, October 12). "Support for Marijuana Legalization Continues to Rise." Pew Research Center. www.pewresearch.org/fact-tank/2016/10/12/support-for-marijuana-legalization-continues-to-rise.

6. Ingraham, C. (2016, March 25). "Support for Marijuana Legalization Has Hit an All-Time High." *Washington Post.* www.washingtonpost.com/news/wonk/wp/2016/03/25/support-for-marijuana-legalization-has-hit-an-all-time-high/?utm_term=.e6b35499d4ae.

7. Bowman, K. (2016, August 12). "Weeding thru Public Opinion on Marijuana." *Forbes.* www.forbes.com/sites/bowmanmarsico/2016/08/12/weeding-thru-public-opinion-on-marijuana/#1a7f66b76af8.

8. Pew Research Center. (2015, April 14). "In Debate over Legalizing Marijuana, Disagreement over Drug's Dangers." www.people-press.org/2015/04/14/in-debate-over-legalizing-marijuana-disagreement-over-drugs-dangers.

9. Berman, M. (2015, February 24). "How Public Opinion on Marijuana Has Changed over the Last Half Century." *Washington Post.* www.washingtonpost.com/news/post-nation/wp/2015/02/24/how-public-opinion-on-marijuana-has-changed-over-the-last-half-century/?utm_term=.24c2837c5b14.

10. Geiger, A. (2016, October 12). "Support for Marijuana Legalization Continues to Rise." Pew Research Center. www.pewresearch.org/fact-tank/2016/10/12/support-for-marijuana-legalization-continues-to-rise.

11. Keyes, K. M., Wall, M., Cerda, M., Schulenberg, J., O'Malley, P. M., Galea, S., Feng, T., & Hasin, D. S. (2016). "How Does State Marijuana Policy Affect U.S. Youth? Medical Marijuana Laws, Marijuana Use and Perceived Harmfulness: 1991–2014." *Society for the Study of Addiction, Addiction Research Report* 111: 2187–95.

12. Subbaraman, M. & Kerr, W. C. (2016). "Marijuana Policy Opinions in Washington State since Legalization: Would Voters Vote the Same Way?" *Contemporary Drug Problems* 43 (4): 369–80.

CHAPTER TWO

1. National Institute on Drug Abuse. www.drugabuse.gov/drugs-abuse/marijuana.

2. Booth, M. (2003). *Cannabis: A History.* New York: St. Martin's Press.

3. Booth, M. (2003). *Cannabis: A History.* New York: St. Martin's Press.

4. McMullin, J. (2005). *Marijuana.* New York: Greenhaven Press.

5. Green, J. (2002). *Cannabis.* New York: Thunder's Mouth Press.

6. McMullin, J. (2005). *Marijuana.* New York: Greenhaven Press.

7. Caulkins, J. P., Hawken, A., Kilmer, B., & Kleiman, M. A. R. (2012). *Marijuana Legalization: What Everyone Needs to Know.* New York: Oxford University Press.

8. Caulkins, J. P., Hawken, A., Kilmer, B., & Kleiman, M. A. R. (2012) *Marijuana Legalization: What Everyone Needs to Know.* New York: Oxford University Press.

9. Allentuck, S. & Bowman, K. M. (2005). "A Clinical Study of the Marijuana High." In McMullin, J. (2005). *Marijuana.* New York: Greenhaven Press, 72–76.

10. Mole, B. (2015, March 24). "Today's Pot Is More Potent, Less Therapeutic." *Science News.* www.sciencenews.org/blog/science-ticker/todday%E2%80%99s-pot-more-potent-less-therapeutic.

11. Caulkins, J. P., Hawken, A., Kilmer, B., & Kleiman, M. A. R. (2012). *Marijuana Legalization: What Everyone Needs to Know.* New York: Oxford University Press.

12. Mole, B. (2015, March 24). "Today's Pot Is More Potent, Less Therapeutic." *Science News.* www.sciencenews.org/blog/science-ticker/todday%E2%80%99s-pot-more-potent-less-therapeutic.

13. Caulkins, J. P., Kilmer, B., Kleiman, M. A., MacCoun, R. J., Midgette, G., Oglesby, P., Pacula, R. L., & Reuter, P. H. (2015). *Considering Marijuana Legalization.* Rand Corporation.

14. Gourdt, C., Giombi, K. C., Kosa, K., Wiley, J. and Cates, S. (2017). "How Four U.S. States Are Regulating Recreational Marijuana Edibles." *International Journal of Drug Policy* 43: 83–90.

15. Caulkins, J. P., Hawken, A., Kilmer, B., & Kleiman, M. A. R. (2012). *Marijuana Legalization: What Everyone Needs to Know.* New York: Oxford University Press.

16. Martinez, M. (2000). *The New Prescription: Marijuana as Medicine.* Oakland: Quick American Archives; Booth, M. (2003). *Cannabis: A History.* New York: St. Martin's Press.

17. "Marijuana History and Timeline." www.concept420.com/information/marijuana-timeline-history; Martinez, M. (2000). *The New Prescription: Marijuana as Medicine.* Oakland: Quick American Archives.

18. Martinez, M. (2000). *The New Prescription: Marijuana as Medicine.* Oakland: Quick American Archives; Rofman, R. A. (1982). *Marijuana as Medicine.* Seattle: Madrona Publishers; Mack, A. & Joy, J. (2001). *Marijuana as Medicine? The Science beyond the Controversy.* Washington, DC: National Academy Press.

19. Dusek, D. E. & Giadano, D. A. (2001). *Drugs: A Factual Account.* New York: McGraw Hill; Joy, J. & Mack, A. (2001). *Marijuana as Medicine? The Science beyond the Controversy.* Washington, DC: National Academy Press.

20. Booth, M. (2003). *Cannabis: A History.* New York: St. Martin's Press.

21. U.S. National Commission on Marijuana and Drug Abuse (1972). "Marijuana: A Signal of Misunderstanding." Druglibrary.org.

22. "Cannabis History." www.cannabissearch.com/history. Robinson, R. (2005). "A Global History of the Hemp Plant." In McMullin, J. (2005). *Marijuana.* New York: Greenhaven Press, 19–29.

23. "History of Marijuana." www.narconon.org/drug-information/marijuana-history.html.

24. Mack, A. & Joy, J. (2001). *Marijuana as Medicine? The Science beyond the Controversy.* Washington, DC: National Academy Press.

25. "Christopher Columbus, Discoverer of the New World: Avid Cannabis User." www.cannabissearch.com/history/christopher-columbus-discoverer-of-the-new-world-avid-cannabis-user.

26. Segal, B. (1986). *Perspectives on Drug Use in the United States.* New York: Haworth Press; Rofman, R. A. (1982). *Marijuana as Medicine.* Seattle: Madrona Publishers.

27. Deitch, R. (2003). *Hemp: American History Revisited: The Plant with a Divided History.* New York: Algora; Booth, M. (2003). *Cannabis: A History.* New York: St. Martin's Press.

28. Thomas Jefferson Foundation (2003). "Spurious Quotations." Monticello. org; Booth, M. (2003). *Cannabis: A History.* New York: St. Martin's Press.

29. "42.0 Milestones in the History of Marijuana." http://brainz.org/420-milestones-history-marijuana.

30. "Marijuana History and Timeline." www.concept420.com/information/marijuana-timeline-history.

31. Grinspoon, L. (1971). *Marijuana Reconsidered.* Cambridge, MA: Harvard University Press; Reinerman, C. (2011). "Cannabis in Cultural and Legal Limbo." In Fraser, S. & Moore, D., eds. *The Drug Effect.* Cambridge: Cambridge University Press, 171–88; Earlywine, M. (2002). *Understanding Marijuana: A New Look at the Scientific Evidence.* New York: Oxford University Press; McMullin, J. (2005). *Marijuana.* New York: Greenhaven Press.

32. Gieringer, D. H. (1999). "The Forgotten Origins of Cannabis Prohibition in California." *Contemporary Drug Problems* 26 (2): 237–89.

33. Green, J. (2002). *Cannabis.* New York: Thunder's Mouth Press.

34. Rappold, R.S. (2014, April 2). "Legalize Medical Marijuana, Doctors Say in Survey." WebMD. www.webmd.com/pain-management/news/20140225/webmd-marijuana-survey-web#1.

35. National Academy of Sciences, Engineering, and Medicine. (2017). *The Health Effects of Cannabis and Cannabinoids: The Current State of Evidence and Recommendations for Research.* Washington, DC: The National Academies Press, 1, 10.

36. Green, J. (2002). *Cannabis.* New York: Thunder's Mouth Press.

37. Whitebread, C. (1995). "The History of the Non-Medical Use of Drugs in the United States." www.drug.library.org/schaffer/History/whiteb1.htm; Booth, M. (2003). *Cannabis: A History.* New York: St. Martin's Press.

38. U.S. Food and Drug Administration. "FDA History—Part I." www.fda.gov/AboutFDA/WhatWeDo/History/Origin/ucm054819.htm; Bonnie, R. J. and Whitebread, C. H. (1999). *The Marijuana Conviction: A History of Marijuana Prohibition in the United States.* New York: The Lindesmith Center.

39. London, J. M. (2009). *How the Use of Marijuana Was Criminalized and Medicalized.* Lewiston, NY: Edwin Mellen; Padwa, H. & Cunningham, J. A. (2010). "Harrison Narcotics Act." In *Addiction: A Reference Encyclopedia.* Santa Barbara, CA: ABC-CLIO.

40. Lee, M. A. (2012). *Smoke Signals: A Social History of Marijuana—Medical, Recreational, and Scientific.* New York: Scribner; Reznicek, M. J. (2012). *Blowing Smoke.* New York: Rowman & Littlefield.

41. Marion, N. E. (2014). *The Medical Marijuana Maze: Policy and Politics.* Durham, NC: Carolina Academic Press; Lee, M. A. (2012). *Smoke Signals: A Social History of Marijuana—Medical, Recreational, and Scientific.* New York: Scribner.

42. Bloomquist, E. R. (1968). *Marijuana.* Beverly Hills, CA: Glencoe Press, 32; Mann, R. (2001). *Grass: The Paged Experience.* Toronto: Warwick Publishing; Newton, D. E. (2013). *Marijuana: A Reference Handbook.* Santa Barbara, CA: ABC-CLIO; Abel, E. L. (2005). "Racism Fuels Fears about Marijuana." In McMullin, J. (2005). *Marijuana.* New York: Greenhaven Press, 52–61.

43. Bonnie, R. & Whitebread II, C. (1999). *The Marijuana Conviction: A History of Marijuana Prohibition in the United States* New York: The Lindesith Center.

44. Mann, R. (2001). *Grass: The Paged Experience.* Toronto: Warwick Publishing.

45. Newton, D. E. (2013). *Marijuana: A Reference Handbook.* Santa Barbara, CA: ABC-CLIO; Anslinger, H. J. (1937). "Marijuana: Assassin of Youth." *American Magazine,* 124, 18–19, 150–53.

46. Carroll, R. (2004). "Under the Influence: Harry Anslinger's Role in Shaping America's Drug Policy." In Erlen, J. & Spillane, J., eds. *Federal Drug Control: The Evolution of Policy and Practice.* Bingham, NY: Haworth Press, 66.

47. Anslinger, H. (1937, July). "Marijuana: Assassin of Youth." *American Magazine,* 124, 1.

48. Fox, S., Armentano, P., & Tvert, M. (2013). *Marijuana Is Safer.* White River Junction, VT: Chelsea Green Publishing, 49.

49. Anslinger, H. & Cooper, C. (1937, July). "Marijuana: Assassin of Youth." *American Magazine,* 124, 150–53.

50. McMullin, J. (2005). *Marijuana.* New York: Greenhaven Press.

51. Hudak, J. (2016). *Marijuana: A Short History.* Washington, DC: Brookings Institution Press, 38.

52. Booth, M. (2003). *Cannabis: A History.* New York: St. Martin's Press.

53. Dusek, D. E. & Gidano, D. A. (1993). *Drugs: A Factual Account.* New York: McGraw Hill; Eddy, M. (2010, April 2). "Medical Marijuana: Review and

Analysis of Federal and State Policies." CRS Report for Congress. www.fas.org/sgp/crs/misc/RL33211.pdf.

54. London, J. M. (2009). *How the Use of Marijuana Was Criminalized and Medicalized.* Lewiston: Edwin Mellen; Padwa, H. & Cunningham, J. A. "Marijuana Tax Act." In *Addiction: A Reference Encyclopedia.* Santa Barbara, CA: ABC-CLIO.

55. The New York Academy of Medicine, the Mayor's Committee on Marijuana. (1944). *The Marihuana Problem in the City of New York.* Lancaster, PA: The Jaques Cattell Press.

56. New York Academy of Medicine. (1955). "Report on Drug Addiction." *Bulletin of the New York Academy of Medicine* 31: 601–7.

57. London, J. M. (2009). *How the Use of Marijuana Was Criminalized and Medicalized.* Lewiston: Edwin Mellen.

58. London, J. M. (2009). *How the Use of Marijuana Was Criminalized and Medicalized.* Lewiston: Edwin Mellen.

59. Bloomquist, E. R. (1968). *Marijuana.* Beverly Hills: Glencoe Press, 37.

60. Lee, M. A. (2012). *Smoke Signals: A Social History of Marijuana—Medical, Recreational, and Scientific.* New York: Scribner; Chasteen, J. C. (2016). *Getting High: Marijuana through the Ages.* New York: Rowman & Littlefield; Bonnie, R. J. & Whitebread III, C. H. (2005). "Marijuana Gains Acceptance." In McMullin, J. (2005). *Marijuana.* New York: Greenhaven Press, 87–100.

61. Marion, N. E. (2014). *The Medical Marijuana Maze.* Durham, NC: Carolina Academic Press.

62. Marion, N. E. (2014). *The Medical Marijuana Maze.* Durham, NC: Carolina Academic Press.

63. Pickerell, J. M. & Chen, P. (2008). "Medical Marijuana Policy and the Virtues of Federalism." *Publius* 38 (1): 22–55.

64. Ogden, D. (2009, October 19). "Memorandum for Selected United States Attorneys." www.justice.gov/sites/default/files/opa/legacy/2009/10/19/medical-marijuana.pdf.

65. U.S. Department of Justice, Office of the Deputy Attorney General. (2011, June 29). "Memorandum for United States Attorneys." www.justice.gov/sites/default/files/oip/legacy/2014/07/23/dag-guidance-2011-for-medical-marijuana-use.pdf.

66. U.S. Department of Justice, Office of the Deputy Attorney General. (2011, June 29). "Memorandum for United States Attorneys." www.justice.gov/sites/default/files/oip/legacy/2014/07/23/dag-guidance-2011-for-medical-marijuana-use.pdf.

67. Cole, J. M. (2013, August 29). "Memorandum for All United States Attorneys." www.justice.gov/iso/opa/resources/3052013829132756857467.pdf.

68. Cole, J. M. (2013, August 29). "Memorandum for All United States Attorneys." www.justice.gov/iso/opa/resources/3052013829132756857467.pdf.

69. U.S. Department of the Treasury, Financial Crimes Enforcement Network. (2014, February 14). "Guidance." www.fincen.gov/sites/default/files/shared/FIN-2014-G001.pdf.

70. U.S. Department of Justice. (2015, February 17). "In Milestone for Sentencing Reform, Attorney General Holder Announces Record Reduction in Mandatory Minimums against Nonviolent Drug Offenders." www.justice.gov/opa/pr/milestone-sentencing-reform-attorney-general-holder-announces-record-reduction-mandatory.

71. Kelly, E., Darke, S., & Ross, J. (2004). "A Review of Drug Use and Driving: Epidemiology, Impairment, Risk Factors, and Risk Perceptions." *Drug and Alcohol Review* 23: 319–44.

72. Anderson, D. M., Hansen, B., & Rees, D. I. (2013). "Medical Marijuana Laws, Traffic Fatalities, and Alcohol Consumption." *The Journal of Law and Economics* 56 (2): 333–69.

73. Shipton, E. A. & Shipton, E. E. (2014). "Should Doctors Be Allowed to Prescribe Cannabinoids for Pain in Australia and New Zealand?" *Australian and New Zealand Journal of Psychiatry* 48: 310–13.

74. Subbaraman, M. & Kerr, W. C. (2016). "Marijuana Policy Opinions in Washington State since Legalization: Would Voters Vote the Same Way?" *Contemporary Drug Problems* 43 (4): 369–80.

CHAPTER THREE

1. Newton, D. E. (2013). *Marijuana: A Reference Handbook.* Santa Barbara, CA: ABC-CLIO.

2. Caulkins, J. P., Hawken, A., Kilmer, B., & Kleiman, M. A. R. (2012). *Marijuana Legalization: What Everyone Needs to Know.* New York: Oxford University Press.

3. Motel, S. (2015, April 14). "6 Facts about Marijuana." Pew Research Center. www.pewresearch.org/fact-tank/2015/04/14/ 6-facts-about-marijuana.

4. National Institute of Health, National Institute on Drug Addiction. "Nationwide Trends." www.drugabuse.gov/publications/drugfacts/nationwide-trends.

5. Centers for Disease Control and Prevention. (2014). "Youth Risk Behavior Surveillance—United States, 2013." *Morbidity and Mortality Weekly Report* 63 (4): 1–170.

6. Johnston, L. D., O'Malley, P. M., Bachman, J. G., & Schulenberg, J. E. (2012). "Monitoring the Future: National Results on Adolescent Drug Use:

Overview of Key Findings." Institute for Social Research, the University of Michigan, Ann Arbor.

7. Substance Abuse and Mental Health Data Archive. "National Survey on Drug Use and Health." (2011). https://datafiles.samhsa.gov/study/national-survey-drug-use-and-health-nsduh-2011-nid13563.

8. St. Pierre, A. (2010, March 28). "Is There Too Much Marijuana on Prime Time TV?" NORML. http://blog.norml.org/2010/03/28/is-there-too-much-marijuana-on-prime-time-tv/; Meslow, S. (2012, April 20). "How TV Fell in Love with Marijuana." *The Atlantic.* www.theatlantic.com/entertainment/archive/2012/04/how-tv-fell-in-love-with-marijuana/256169.

9. Steinhauer, J. (2002, April 10). "Bloomberg Says He Regrets Marijuana Remarks." *New York Times.*

10. Schneider, S. K., Jacoby, W. G., & Lewis, D. C. (2011). "Public Opinion toward Intergovernmental Policy Responsibilities." *Publius* 41 (1): 1–30; Dahl, R. A. (1956). *A Preface to Democratic Theory.* Chicago: University of Chicago Press.; Wright, G. C., Ericson, R. S., & McIver, J. P. (1987). "Public Opinion and Policy Liberalism in the American States." *American Journal of Political Science* 31 (4): 980–1001.

11. Schneider, S. K., Jacoby, W. G., & Lewis, D. C. (2011). "Public Opinion toward Intergovernmental Policy Responsibilities." *Publius* 41 (1): 1–30.

12. Cook, F. L., Barabas, J., & Page, B. I. (2002). "Invoking Public Opinion: Policy Elites and Social Security." *American Association for Public Opinion Research* 66 (2): 235–64; Schneider, S. K., Jacoby, W. G., & Lewis, D. C. (2011). "Public Opinion toward Intergovernmental Policy Responsibilities." *Publius* 41 (1): 1–30; Lax, J. R. & Phillips, J. H. (2009). "Gay Rights in the States: Public Opinion and Policy Responsiveness." *The American Political Science Review* 103 (3): 367–86; Page, B. I. (1994). "Democratic Responsiveness? Untangling the Links between Public Opinion and Policy." *Political Science and Politics* 27 (1) 25–29; Page, B. I. & Shapiro, R. Y. (1983). "Effects of Public Opinion on Policy." *The American Political Science Review.* 77 (1): 175–90.

13. Weber, R. E. & Shaffer, W. R. (1972). "Public Opinion and American State Policy-Making." *Midwest Journal of Political Science* 16 (4): 683–99.

14. Monroe, A. D. (1979). "Consistency between Public Preferences and National Policy Decisions." *American Politics Quarterly* 7: 3–19; Hartley, T. & Russett, B. (1992). "Public Opinion and the Common Defense: Who Governs Military Spending in the United States?" *American Political Science Review* 86: 905–15; Page, B. I. & Shapiro, R. Y. (1983). "Effects of Public Opinion on Policy." *The American Political Science Review* 77 (1): 175–90; Stimson, J. A., MacKuen, M. B., & Eriksen, R. S. (1995). "Dynamic Representation." *American Political Science Review* 89 (3): 543–65; Wlezien, C. (1995). "The Public as

Thermostat: Dynamics of Preferences for Spending." *American Journal of Political Science* 39 (4): 981–1000; Weber, R. E. & Shaffer, W. R. (1972). "Public Opinion and American State Policy-Making." *Midwest Journal of Political Science* 16 (4): 694–95.

15. Erickson, R. S. (1976). "The Relationship between Public Opinion and State Policy: A New Look Based on Some Forgotten Data." *American Journal of Political Science* 20 (1): 25–36.

16. Monroe, A. D. (1998). "Public Opinion and Public Policy, 1980–1993." *The Public Opinion Quarterly* 62 (1): 6–28; Page, B. I. & Shapiro, R. Y. (1983). "Effects of Public Opinion on Policy." *The American Political Science Review* 77 (1): 175–90.

17. Page, B. I. & Shapiro, R. Y. (1983). "Effects of Public Opinion on Policy." *The American Political Science Review.* 77 (1): 189.

18. Burstein, P. (2003). "The Impact of Public Opinion on Public Policy: A Review and an Agenda." *Political Research Quarterly* 56 (1): 29–40.

19. Agnone, J. (2007). "Amplifying Public Opinion: The Policy Impact of the U.S. Environmental Movement." *Social Forces.* 85 (4): 1593–620.

20. Lax, J. R. & Phillips, J. H. (2009). "Gay Rights in the States: Public Opinion and Policy Responsiveness." *The American Political Science Review* 103 (3): 370.

21. Lax, J. R. & Phillips, J. H. (2009). "Gay Rights in the States: Public Opinion and Policy Responsiveness." *The American Political Science Review* 103 (3): 367–86.

22. Wetstein, M. E. & Albritton, R. B. (1995). "Effects of Public Opinion on Abortion Policies and Use in the American States." *Publius* 25 (4): 104.

23. Page, B. I. & Shapiro, R. Y. (1983). "Effects of Public Opinion on Policy." *The American Political Science Review.* 77 (1): 175–90.

24. Cook, F. L., Barabas, J., & Page, B. I. (2002). "Invoking Public Opinion: Policy Elites and Social Security." *American Association for Public Opinion Research* 66 (2): 235–64.

25. Mayhew, D. (1974). *Congress: The Electoral Connection.* New Haven, CT: Yale University Press; Wright, G. C., Ericson, R. S, & McIver, J. P. (1987). "Public Opinion and Policy Liberalism in the American States." *American Journal of Political Science* 31 (4): 980–1001.

26. Nixon, R. M. (March 14, 1973). "State of the Union Message to the Congress on Law Enforcement and Drug Abuse Prevention." The American Presidency Project. www.presidency.ucsb.edu/ws/?pid=4140.

27. Martinez, M. (2000). *The New Prescription: Marijuana as Medicine.* Oakland: Quick American Archives.

28. Nixon, R. M. (March 10, 1973). "Radio Address about the State of the Union Message on Law Enforcement and Drug Abuse Prevention." The American Presidency Project. www.presidency.ucsb.edu/ws/?pid=4135.

29. U.S. Commission on Marijuana and Drug Abuse. (1972). *Marijuana: A Signal of Misunderstanding.* Washington, DC: U.S. Government Printing Office.

30. Hudak, J. (2016). *Marijuana: A Short History.* Washington, D.C.: Brookings Institution Press; Rendon, J. (2012). *Super-Charged.* Portland: Timber Press.

31. Ford, G. R. (September 16, 1975). "The President's News Conference." The American Presidency Project. www.presidency.ucsb.edu/ws/?pid=5255.

32. Martinez, M. (2000). *The New Prescription: Marijuana as Medicine.* Oakland: Quick American Archives.

33. Wodak, A., Reinarman, C., & Cohen, P. D. A. (2005). "The Pros and Cons of Marijuana Legalization." In McMullin, J. (2005). *Marijuana.* New York: Greenhaven Press, 132–40.

34. Booth, M. (2003). *Cannabis: A History.* New York: St. Martin's Press.

35. Reagan, R. R. (June 24, 1982). "Remarks on Signing Executive Order 12368 Concerning Federal Drug Abuse Policy Functions." The American Presidency Project. www.presidency.ucsb.edu/ws/?pid=42671.

36. Reagan, R. R. (June 30, 1984). "Radio Address to the Nation on Drug Abuse." The American Presidency Project. www.presidency.ucsb.edu/ws/?pid=40117.

37. Reagan, R. R. (March 16, 1983). "Message to the Congress Transmitting Proposed Crime Control Legislation." The American Presidency Project. www.presidency.ucsb.edu/ws/?pid=41058.

38. Booth, M. (2003). *Cannabis: A History.* New York: St. Martin's Press.

39. Bush, G. H. W. (September 5, 1989). "Address to the Nation on the National Drug Control Strategy." The American Presidency Project. www.presidency.ucsb.edu/ws/?pid=17472.

40. Bush, G. H. W. (September 6, 1989). "The President's News Conference on the National Drug Control Strategy." The American Presidency Project. www.presidency.ucsb.edu/ws/?pid=17475.

41. Bush, G. H. W. (February 26, 1992). "Remarks at the State Dinner for Drug Summit Participants in San Antonio." The American Presidency Project. www.presidency.ucsb.edu/ws/?pid=20652.

42. Bush, George H. W. (February 13, 1990). "Remarks on Signing the United Nations Convention against Illegal Traffic in Narcotic Drugs and Psychotropic Substances." The American Presidency Project. www.presidency.ucsb.edu/ws/?pid=18148.

43. Clark, P. A. (2000). "The Ethics of Medical Marijuana: Government Restrictions vs. Medical Necessity." *Journal of Public Health Policy* 21 (1): 41.

44. Claiborne, W. (1997, January 1). "Federal Warning on Medical Marijuana Leaves Physicians Feeling Intimidated." *Washington Post*, A6.

45. Hudak, J. (2016). *Marijuana: A Short History.* Washington, DC: Brookings Institution Press, 83.

46. Hudak, J. (2016). *Marijuana: A Short History.* Washington, DC: Brookings Institution Press, 83–84.

47. Kreit, A. (2003). "The Future of Medical Marijuana: Should the States Grow Their Own?" *University of Pennsylvania Law Review* 151 (5): 1787–826: 1789–790.

48. Gerber, R. (2004). *Legalizing Marijuana: Drug Policy Reform and Prohibition Politics.* Westport, CT: Praeger, 133.

49. Obama, B. (2011, September 26). "Remarks at a Democratic National Committee Fundraiser in West Hollywood, California." The American Presidency Project. www.presidency.ucsb.edu/ws/?pid=96812.

50. Johnston, D. & Lewis, N. A. (2009, March 18). "Obama Administration to Stop Raids on Medical Marijuana Dispensers." *New York Times*, A20, www.nytimes.com/2009/03/19/us/19holder.html.

51. Cole, J. M. (2013, August 29). "Memorandum for All United States Attorneys." www.justice.gov/iso/opa/resources/3052013829132756857467.pdf.

52. Horwitz, S. (2017, May 9). "Sessions Weighs Return to Harsher Punishments for Low-Level Drug Crimes." *Washington Post.* www.washingtonpost.com/world/national-security/sessions-reviews-justice-department-criminal-charging-policy/2017/05/09/74ffac3a-2e8d-11e7-8674-437ddb6e813e_story.html.

53. Savage, D. (2016, March 21). "Supreme Court Rejects Challenge to Colorado Marijuana Law from Other States." *Los Angeles Times.* www.latimes.com/nation/la-na-court-marijuana-states-20160321-story.html.

CHAPTER FOUR

1. Newton, D. E. (2013). *Marijuana: A Reference Handbook.* Santa Barbara, CA: ABC-CLIO.

2. "10 Little-Known Facts in the Medical Marijuana Debate." http://medicalmarijuana.procon.org/view.resource.php?resourceID=004289.

3. Armentano, P. (2012, July 29). "Five Scientific Conclusions about Cannabis That the Mainstream Media Doesn't Want You to Know." www.alternet.org/

drugs/five-scientific-conclusions-about-cannabis--mainstream--media--doesn't--want--you--to--know.

4. National Academies of Sciences, Engineering, and Medicine (2017). *The Health Effects of Cannabis and Cannabinoids.* Washington, DC: National Academies Press.

5. Bechtold, J., Simpson, T., White, H. R., & Pardini, D. (2015). "Chronic Adolescent Marijuana Use as a Risk Factor for Physical and Mental Health Problems in Young Adult Men." *Psychology of Addictive Behaviors* 29 (3): 552–63.

6. Madras, B. K. (2015). "20 Flaws in Study Finding No Health Problems in Adult Males Who Were Chronic Marijuana Users as Teens, Young Adults." *The Journal of Global Drug Policy and Practice* 9 (3): 1–21.

7. Callaghan, R. C., Allebeck, P., & Sidorchuk, A. (2013, October). "Marijuana Use and Risk of Lung Cancer: A 40 Year Cohort Study." *Cancer Causes Control* 24: 1811–20.

8. National Institute of Health, National Institute on Drug Abuse. (April 2017). "What Are Marijuana's Effects on Lung Health?" www.drugabuse.gov/publications/marijuana/what-are-marijuanas-effects-lung-health; DiLascio, T. M. (2014). "Reform—The Marijuana Legalization Debate." In *The Reference Shelf: Marijuana Reform.* Ipswich, MA: Grey House Publishing, 3–7.

9. Wodak, A., Reinarman, C., & Cohen, P. D. A. (2005). "The Pros and Cons of Marijuana Legalization." In McMullin, J. (2005). *Marijuana.* New York: Greenhaven Press, 132–40.

10. National Institute of Health, National Institute on Drug Abuse. (2017, April). "What Are Marijuana's Long-Term Effects on the Brain?" www.drugabuse.gov/publications/marijuana/what-are-marijuanas-long-term-effects-brain.

11. Solowij, N. (January 2008). "Cognitive Functioning of Long-Term Heavy Cannabis Users Seeking Treatment." *Journal of the American Medical Association* 1 (1): 98.

12. National Institute of Health, National Institute on Drug Abuse. (2017, April). "What Are Marijuana's Long-Term Effects on the Brain?" www.drugabuse.gov/publications/marijuana/what-are-marijuanas-long-term-effects-brain.

13. Smith, M. J., Cobia, D. J., Wang. L, Alpert, K., Cronenwett, W. J., Goldman, M. B., Mamah, D., Barch, D. M., Breiter, H., Csernansky, J. G., & Cobia, D. J. (2013). "Cannabis-Related Working Memory Deficits and Associated Subcortical Morphological Differences in Healthy Individuals and Schizophrenia Subjects." *Schizophrenia Bulletin* 40 (2): 287–99.

14. National Academies of Sciences, Engineering, and Medicine (2017). *The Health Effects of Cannabis and Cannabinoids.* Washington, DC: National Academies Press.

15. Fields, R. D. (2009). "Marijuana Hurts Some, Helps Others." *Scientific American Mind* 20 (5): 17.

16. Sanders, L. (2015, December 16). "Brain Damage Seen in Potent-Marijuana Smokers." *Science News for Students.* www.sciencenewsforstudents.org/article/brain-damage-seen-potent-marijuana-smokers.

17. Shively, R. (2016). "Marijuana Legalization: Policy Ahead of Science." *Journal of Community Corrections* 26 (1): 9–11.

18. Allentuck, S. & Bowman, K. M. (2005). "A Clinical Study of the Marijuana High." In McMullin, J. (2005). *Marijuana.* New York: Greenhaven Press, 72–76.

19. Williamson, J. L., Buckland, H. T., & Cunningham, S. L. (2013, April). "How Does Marijuana Work in the Brain?" *The American Biology Teacher* 75 (4): 299–300.

20. National Institute of Health, National Institute on Drug Abuse. (2017, April). "What Are Marijuana's Long-Term Effects on the Brain?" www.drugabuse.gov/publications/marijuana/what-are-marijuanas-long-term-effects-brain.

21. Madras, B. K. (2015). "20 Flaws in Study Finding No Health Problems in Adult Males Who Were Chronic Marijuana Users as Teens, Young Adults." *The Journal of Global Drug Policy and Practice* 9 (3): 1–21.

22. National Academies of Sciences, Engineering, and Medicine (2017). *The Health Effects of Cannabis and Cannabinoids.* Washington, DC: National Academies Press.

23. National Institute of Health, National Institute on Drug Abuse. (2017, February). "Drug Facts: What Is Marijuana?" www.drugabuse.gov/publications/drugfacts/marijuana.

24. Patton, G. C., Coffey, C., Carlin, J. B., Lynskey, M., & Hall, W. (2002). "Cannabis Use and Mental Health in Young People: Cohort Study." *British Medical Journal* 325: 7374.

25. Green, B. E. & Ritter, C. (2000). "Marijuana Use and Depression." *Journal of Health and Social Behavior* 41 (1): 40–49.

26. National Academies of Sciences, Engineering, and Medicine (2017). *The Health Effects of Cannabis and Cannabinoids.* Washington, DC: National Academies Press.

27. National Academies of Sciences, Engineering, and Medicine (2017). *The Health Effects of Cannabis and Cannabinoids.* Washington, DC: National Academies Press.

28. National Academies of Sciences, Engineering, and Medicine (2017). *The Health Effects of Cannabis and Cannabinoids.* Washington, DC: National Academies Press.

29. Sanders, L. (2014, August 9). "Frequent Marijuana Use May Affect Dopamine Response." *Science News* 186 (3): 20.

30. Newton, D. E. (2013). *Marijuana: A Reference Handbook.* Santa Barbara, CA: ABC-CLIO; National Institute on Drug Abuse, National Institute of Health. "InfoFact: Marijuana." www.drugabuse.gov/publications/infofacts/marijuana.

31. Madras, B. K. (2015). "20 Flaws in Study Finding No Health Problems in Adult Males Who Were Chronic Marijuana Users as Teens, Young Adults." *The Journal of Global Drug Policy and Practice* 9 (3): 3; Middlebrook, H. (2016, November 14). "Does Marijuana Weaken Heart Muscles?" CNN Health. www.cnn.com/2016/11/13/health/marijuana-weakens-heart/index.html; Beil, L. (2016, November 14). "Marijuana Use Weakens Heart Muscle." *Science News.* www.sciencenews.org/article/marijuana-use-weakens-heart-muscle.

32. National Academies of Sciences, Engineering, and Medicine (2017). *The Health Effects of Cannabis and Cannabinoids.* Washington, DC: National Academies Press.

33. Madras, B. K. (2015). "20 Flaws in Study Finding No Health Problems in Adult Males Who Were Chronic Marijuana Users as Teens, Young Adults." *The Journal of Global Drug Policy and Practice* 9 (3): 3; National Academies of Sciences, Engineering, and Medicine. (2017). *The Health Effects of Cannabis and Cannabinoids.* Washington, DC: National Academies Press.

34. Hudak, J. (2016). *Marijuana: A Short History.* Washington, DC: Brookings Institution Press.

35. National Academies of Sciences, Engineering, and Medicine. (2017). *The Health Effects of Cannabis and Cannabinoids.* Washington, DC: National Academies Press.

36. Bluhm, E. C., Daniels, J., Pollock, B. H., Olshan, A. F. (2006). "Maternal Use of Recreational Drugs and Neuroblastoma in Offspring: A Report from the Children's Oncology Group." *Cancer Causes and Control* 17 (5): 663–69.

37. National Academies of Sciences, Engineering, and Medicine (2017). *The Health Effects of Cannabis and Cannabinoids.* Washington, DC: National Academies Press.

38. National Institute of Health, National Institute on Drug Abuse. (2017, April). "What Are Marijuana's Effects on Other Aspects of Physical Health?" www.drugabuse.gov/publications/research-reports/marijuana/what-are-marijuana%E2%80%99s-effects-on-other-aspects-of-physical-health%3F; National Academies of Sciences, Engineering, and Medicine (2017). *The Health Effects of Cannabis and Cannabinoids.* Washington, DC: National Academies Press.

39. Drug Policy Alliance. "Is It True That Marijuana Has Medicinal Qualities?" www.drugpolicy.org/drug-facts/10-facts-about-marijuana/marijuana-medicinal-properties.

40. Seppa, N. (2015, April 13). "Marijuana Component Fights Epilepsy." *Science News*. www.sciencenews.org/article/marijuana-component-fights-epilepsy.

41. Cha, A. E. (2018). "Marijuana-Based Anti-Seizure Drug Could Hit U.S. Market in 2018 after Strong Study Results." *Washington Post*. www.washingtonpost. com/news/to-your-health/wp/2018/01/24/marijuana-based-anti-seizure-drug-may-hit-u-s-market-in-2018-after-strong-study-results/?noredirect=on&utm_ term=.62c5b9026bf6.

42. Noonan, D. (2017, May 25). "Marijuana Treatment Reduces Severe Epileptic Seizures." *Scientific American*. www.scientificamerican.com/article/ marijuana-treatment-reduces-severe-epileptic-seizures.

43. National Institute of Health, National Institute on Drug Abuse. (2017). "What Is Medical Marijuana?" www.drugabuse.gov/publications/drugfacts/ marijuana-medicine; Drug Policy Alliance. "10 Facts about Marijuana." www. drugpolicy.org/drug-facts/10-facts-about-marijuana/marijuana-gateway-drug.

44. National Academies of Sciences, Engineering, and Medicine (2017). *The Health Effects of Cannabis and Cannabinoids*. Washington, DC: National Academies Press.

45. Levine, D. (2014). "Medical Marijuana: 4 Experts on Benefits versus Risks." In *The Reference Shelf: Marijuana Reform*. Ipswich, MA: Grey House Publishing, 1343–47; Wodak, A., Reinarman, C., & Cohen, P. D. A. (2005). "The Pros and Cons of Marijuana Legalization." In McMullin, J. (2005). *Marijuana*. New York: Greenhaven Press, 132–40.

46. Miller, N. S. & Oberbarnscheidt, T. (2017). "Health Policy for Marijuana." *The Journal of Global Drug Policy and Practice* 11 (3): 28–61.

47. Levine, D. (2014). "Medical Marijuana: 4 Experts on Benefits versus Risks." In *The Reference Shelf: Marijuana Reform*. Ipswich, MA: Grey House Publishing, 1343–47.

48. National Academies of Sciences, Engineering, and Medicine. (2017, January 12). "The Health Effects of Cannabis and Cannabinoids." www.nap.edu.

49. Wodak, A., Reinarman, C., & Cohen, P. D. A. (2005). "The Pros and Cons of Marijuana Legalization." In McMullin, J. (2005). *Marijuana*. New York: Greenhaven Press, 139.

50. American College of Physicians. (2017, September 5). "Benefits and Harms of Plant-Based Cannabis for Posttraumatic Stress Disorder: A Systematic Review." *Annals of Internal Medicine*. http://annals.org/aim/fullarticle/2648596/ benefits-harms-plant-based-cannabis-posttraumatic-stress-disorder-systematic-review.

51. American College of Physicians. (2017, September 5). "The Effects of Cannabis among Adults with Chronic Pain and an Overview of General Harms: A Systematic Review." *Annals of Internal Medicine*. http://annals.org/aim/fullar-

ticle/2648595/effects--cannabis-among-adults-chronic-pain-overview-general-harms-systematic.

52. National Academies of Sciences, Engineering, and Medicine. (2017). "The Health Effects of Cannabis and Cannabinoids." Washington, DC: National Academies Press, 90.

53. Miller, N. S. & Oberbarnscheidt, T. (2017). "Health Policy for Marijuana." *The Journal of Global Drug Policy and Practice* 11 (3): 28–61.

54. National Families in Action. "What Will Legal Marijuana Cost Employees?" http://drugfreebusiness.org/Media/documents/What%20Will%20Legal%20Marijuana%20Cost%20Employers--Complete.pd.pdf.

55. DiLascio, T. M. (2014). "Reform—The Marijuana Legalization Debate." In *The Reference Shelf: Marijuana Reform.* Ipswich, MA: Grey House Publishing, 3–7.

56. National Institute of Health, National Institute on Drug Abuse. (2017, February). "What Is Marijuana?" www.drugabuse.gov/publications/drugfacts/marijuana.

57. Caulkins, J. P., Hawken, A., Kilmer, B., & Kleiman, M. A. R. (2012). *Marijuana Legalization: What Everyone Needs to Know* (New York: Oxford University Press).

58. FDSA Office of Pharmacoepidemiology and Statistical Science. (2005). "Adverse Event Reporting System (AERS) Brief Description with Caveats of System." http://medicalmarijuana.procon.org/sourcefiles/fdaaers.pdf; "Medical Marijuana: Pharmaceutical Drugs Based on Cannabis." http://mecicalmarijuana.procon.org/view.resource.php?resourceID=000883.

59. Clark, J. (2017, November 16). "Colorado Doctors Say 11-Month-old Died from Marijuana Overdose." NBC4. www.nbc4i.com/news/u-s-world/colorado-doctors-say-11-month-old-died-from-marijuana-overdose/1096273844; Silverman, E. (2017, November 17). "The Truth behind the 'First' Marijuana Overdose Death' Headlines." *The Washington Post.* www.washingtonpost.com/news/to-your-health/wp/2017/11/17/the-truth-behind-the-first-marijuana-overdose-death/?utm_term=.a1afadbfcd35.

60. National Institute of Health, National Institute on Drug Abuse. (2017, February). "What Is Marijuana?" www.drugabuse.gov/publications/drugfacts/marijuana; Hudak, J. (2016). *Marijuana: A Short History.* Washington, DC: Brookings Institution Press; Drug Policy Alliance. "10 Facts about Marijuana." www.drugpolicy.org/drug-facts/10-facts-about-marijuana/marijuana-how-strong.

61. National Academies of Sciences, Engineering, and Medicine (2017). *The Health Effects of Cannabis and Cannabinoids.* Washington, DC: National Academies Press.

62. Brangham, W. (2014). "Is Pot Getting More Potent?" In *The Reference Shelf: Marijuana Reform*. Ipswich, MA: Grey House Publishing, 159–61; Holland, J. (2010). *The Pot Book: A Complete Guide to Cannabis*. Rochester, VT: Park Street Press; Hellerman, C. (2013, August 9). "Is Super Weed, Super Bad?" CNN. www.cnn.com/2013/08/09/health/weed-potency-levels; Hudak, J. (2016). *Marijuana: A Short History*. Washington, DC: Brookings Institution Press, 18.

63. Allentuck, S. & Bowman, K. M. (2005). "A Clinical Study of the Marijuana High." In McMullin, J. (2005). *Marijuana*. New York: Greenhaven Press, 72–76.

64. Room, R.; Fisher, B., Hall, W., Lenton, S., & Reuter, P. (2010). *Cannabis Policy: Moving beyond Stalemate*. New York: Oxford University Press.

65. Caulkins, J. P., Hawken, A., Kilmer, B., & Kleiman, M. A. R. (2012). *Marijuana Legalization: What Everyone Needs to Know*. New York: Oxford University Press.

66. National Academies of Sciences, Engineering, and Medicine (2017). *The Health Effects of Cannabis and Cannabinoids*. Washington, DC: National Academies Press.

67. Lee, S. S., Humphreys, K. L., Flory, K., Liu, R., & Glass, K. (2011). "Prospective Association of Childhood Attention-Deficit/Hyperactivity Disorder (ADHD) and Substance Use and Abuse/Dependence: A Meta-Analytic Review." *Clinical Psychology Review* 31 (3): 328–41.

68. Barclay, R. S. (2016, August 9). "Marijuana Addiction Is Rare, but Very Real." Healthline. www.healthline.com/health-news/marijuana-addiction-rare-but-real-072014#1.

69. Levine, D. (2014). "Medical Marijuana: 4 Experts on Benefits versus Risks." In *The Reference Shelf: Marijuana Reform*. Ipswich, MA: Grey House Publishing, 134–37.

70. "Cannabinoids: Reward, Dependence, and Underlying Neurochemical Mechanisms—A Review of Recent Preclinical Data." (2003) *Psychopharmacology* 169 (2): 115–34.

71. California Society of Addiction Medicine. (2009, September). "Impact of Marijuana on Children and Adolescents: Evidence-Based Information on Cannabis/Marijuana." San Francisco, CA.

72. Wodak, A., Reinarman, C., & Cohen, P. D. A. (2005). "The Pros and Cons of Marijuana Legalization." In McMullin, J. (2005). *Marijuana*. New York: Greenhaven Press, 132–40.

73. Substance Abuse and Mental Health Services Administration, Office of Applied Studies. "Treatment Episode Data Set (TEDS): 2009 Discharges from Substance Abuse Treatment Services."

74. Maier, S. L., Mannes, S., & Koppenhofer, E. L. (2017). "The Implications of Marijuana Decriminalization and Legalization on Crime in the United States." *Contemporary Drug Problems* 44 (2): 125–46.

75. Shepard, E. M. & Blackley, P. R. (2016). "Medical Marijuana and Crime: Further Evidence from the Western States." *Journal of Drug Issues* 46 (2): 122–34.

76. Caulkins, J. P., Hawken, A. Kilmer, B., & Kleiman, M. A. R. (2012). *Marijuana Legalization: What Everyone Needs to Know*. New York: Oxford University Press.

77. Miron, J. A. (2010, February). "The Budgetary Implications of Drug Prohibition." http://scholar.harvard.edu/files/miron/files/budget_2010_final_0.pdf.

78. Vonvwef, J. (2018, January 15). "Marijuana Legalization Causing Violent Crime to Fall in US States, Study Finds." *Independent*. www.independent.co.uk/news/world/americas/medical-marijuana-legislation-cannabis-us-states-violent-crime-drop-numbers-study-california-new-a816031; Doward, Jamie (2018, January 13). "Legal Marijuana Cuts Violence Says US Study, as Medical-Use Laws See Crime Fall." *Guardian*. www.theguardian.com/world/2018/jan/14/legal-marijuana-medical-use-crime-rate-plummets-us-study.

79. DiLascio, T. M. (2014). "Reform—The Marijuana Legalization Debate." In *The Reference Shelf: Marijuana Reform*. Ipswich, MA: Grey House Publishing, 3–7.

80. Hotakainen, R. (2013, May 23). "Marijuana Is Drug Most Often Linked to Crime, Study Finds." McClatchy Washington Bureau. www.mcclatchydc.com/news/politics-goverment/article24749413.html.

81. Fields, R. D. (2016, March 20). "Marijuana Use Increases Violent Behavior." *Psychology Today*. www.psychologytoday.com/us/blog/the-new-brain/201603/marijuana-use-increases-violent-behavior.

82. Freisthler, B., Gruenewald, P. J., & Wolf, J. P. (2015). "Examining the Relationship between Marijuana Use, Medical Marijuana Dispensaries, and Abusive and Neglectful Parenting." *Child Abuse and Neglect* 48: 170–78.

83. Caulkins, J. P., Hawken, A., Kilmer, B., & Kleiman, M. A. R. (2012). *Marijuana Legalization: What Everyone Needs to Know*. New York: Oxford University Press.

84. Carise, D. (2013, July 23). "Legalizing Marijuana—The Real Costs." Huffington Post. www.huffingtonpost.com/deni-carise/legalizing-marijuana-the-_b_3620472.html.

85. National Institute of Health, National Institute of Drug Abuse. "Is Marijuana a Gateway Drug?" www.drugabuse.gov/publications/research-reports/marijuana/marijuana-gateway-drug; National Institute of Health, National Institute of Drug Abuse. (2017, April). "What Are Marijuana's Long-Term Effects on the

Brain?" www.drugabuse.gov/publications/marijuana/what-are-marijuanas-long-term-effects-brain.

86. American Council for Drug Education. "Basic Facts about Drugs." www.acde.org/common/Marijuana.htm.

87. National Academies of Sciences, Engineering, and Medicine (2017). *The Health Effects of Cannabis and Cannabinoids.* Washington, DC: National Academies Press.

88. Subbaraman, M. & Kerr, W. C. (2016). "Marijuana Policy Opinions in Washington State since Legalization: Would Voters Vote the Same Way?" *Contemporary Drug Problems* 43 (4): 378.

89. Subbaraman, M. & Kerr, W. C. (2016). "Marijuana Policy Opinions in Washington State since Legalization: Would Voters Vote the Same Way?" *Contemporary Drug Problems* 43 (4): 369–80.

90. Damrongplasit, K., Hsiao, C., & Zhao, X. (2010). "Decriminalization and Marijuana Smoking Prevalence: Evidence from Australia." *Journal of Business & Economic Statistics.* 28 (3): 344–356.

91. Wodak, A., Reinarman, C., & Cohen, P. D. A. (2005). "The Pros and Cons of Marijuana Legalization." In McMullin, J. (2005). *Marijuana.* New York: Greenhaven Press, 132–40.

92. Kilmer, B., Caulkins, J. P., Bond, B. M., & Reuter, P. H. (2010). "Reducing Drug Trafficking Revenues and Violence in Mexico." Rand Corporation.

93. DiLascio, T. M. (2014). "Reform—The Marijuana Legalization Debate." In *The Reference Shelf: Marijuana Reform.* Ipswich, MA: Grey House Publishing, 3–7.

94. Van Gerpen, S., Vik, T., & Soundy, T. J. (2015). "Medicinal and Recreational Marijuana: What Are the Risks?" *South Dakota Medicine Special Edition*: 58–62.

95. Bach, J. (2017, May 26). "Where the Marijuana Taxes Will Go: Economists Estimate $210M Payout from Oregon Pot Sales." *Statesman Journal.* www.oregon.gov/das/OEA/Documents/forecast0517.pdf.

96. "Marijuana Is Top U.S. Cash Crop, Pro-Legalization Analysis Says." *Los Angeles Times.* December 18. 2006.

97. "Marijuana Is Top U.S. Cash Crop, Pro-Legalization Analysis Says." *Los Angeles Times.* December 18. 2006.

98. Gettman, J. (2007). "Lost Taxes and Other Costs of Marijuana Laws." DrugScience.org.

99. "Cannabis 101: A Practical Guide for the New Consumer." Leafly.com.

100. Caulkins, J. P., Kilmer, B., Kleiman, M. A. R., MacCoun, R. J., Midgette, G., Oglesby, M., Pacula, R. L., & Reuter, P. H. (2015). "Taxation and Other Sources of Revenue." Rand Corporation.

101. Evans, D. G. (2012, October 30). "Marijuana's Legalization's Costs Outweigh Its Benefits." *U.S. News and World Report.* www.usnews.com/debate-club/should-marijuana-use-be-legalized/marijuana-legalizations-costs-outweigh-its-benefits; Carise, D. (July 23, 2013). "Legalizing Marijuana—The Real Costs." Huffington Post. www.huffingtonpost.com/deni-carise/legalizing-marijuana-the-_b_3620472.html.

102. Wodak, A., Reinarman, C., & Cohen, P. D. A. (2005). "The Pros and Cons of Marijuana Legalization." In McMullin, J. (2005). *Marijuana.* New York: Greenhaven Press, 132–40.

CHAPTER EIGHT

1. Charmaz, K. (2014). *Constructing Grounded Theory.* London: Sage.

CHAPTER NINE

1. Griffin III, O. H., Fritsch, A. L., Woodward, V. H., & Mohn, R. S. (2013). "Sifting through the Hyperbole: One Hundred Years of Marijuana Coverage in the *New York Times.*" *Deviant Behavior* 34 (10): 767–81.

2. Mills, C. W. (2000). *The Sociological Imagination.* Oxford: Oxford University Press.

3. Weitzer, R. (2012). *Legalizing Prostitution: From Illicit Vice to Lawful Business.* New York: New York University Press.

4. Seidman, S. (2016). *Contested Knowledge: Social Theory Today.* West Sussex, UK: John Wiley & Sons, Ltd.

5. Meja, V. & Stehr, N. (Eds.). (2014). *Knowledge and Politics (RLE Social Theory): The Sociology of Knowledge Dispute.* London: Routledge.

6. Schiappa, E. (1993). "Arguing about Definitions." *Argumentation* 7 (4): 403–17.

7. Beck, U. (1992). *Risk Society: Towards a New Modernity.* Thousand Oaks, CA: Sage.

8. Giddens, A. (1991). *Modernity and Self-Identity: Self and Society in the Late Modern Age.* Stanford, CA: Stanford University Press.

9. Giddens, A. (1991). *Modernity and Self-identity: Self and Society in the Late Modern Age.* Stanford, CA: Stanford University Press.

10. Beck, U. (1992). *Risk Society: Towards a New Modernity.* Thousand Oaks, CA: Sage.

11. Young, J. (1999). *The Exclusive Society.* Thousand Oaks, CA: Sage; Young, J. (2011). *The Criminological Imagination.* Cambridge: Polity Press.

12. Fox, S., Armentano, P., & Tvert, P. (2013). *Marijuana Is Safer: So Why Are We Driving People to Drink?* White River Junction, VT: Chelsea Green Publishing.

13. Young, J. (1999). *The Exclusive Society.* Thousand Oaks, CA: Sage; Young, J. (2011). *The Criminological Imagination.* Cambridge: Polity Press; Young, J. (2007). *The Vertigo of Late Modernity.* Los Angeles: Sage.

14. Young, J. (1999). *The Exclusive Society.* Thousand Oaks, CA: Sage; Young, J. (2011). *The Criminological Imagination.* Cambridge: Polity Press; Young, J. (2007). *The Vertigo of Late Modernity.* Los Angeles: Sage.

15. Young, J. (1999). *The Exclusive Society.* Thousand Oaks, CA: Sage; Young, J. (2011). *The Criminological Imagination.* Cambridge: Polity Press; Young, J. (2007). *The Vertigo of Late Modernity.* Los Angeles: Sage.

16. Young, J. (1999). *The Exclusive Society.* Thousand Oaks, CA: Sage; Young, J. (2011). *The Criminological Imagination.* Cambridge: Polity Press; Young, J. (2007). *The Vertigo of Late Modernity.* Los Angeles: Sage.

17. Young, J. (1999). *The Exclusive Society.* Thousand Oaks, CA: Sage.

18. Roseneil, S. & Seymour, J. (1999). "Practising Identities: Power and Resistance." In *Practising Identities.* London: Palgrave, 1–10.

CHAPTER TEN

1. Lakoff, G. (1987). *Women, Fire, and Dangerous Things: What Categories Reveal about the Mind.* Chicago: University of Chicago Press.

2. Hill, J. B. & Banks, J. (2018). "Bitches, Fishes, and Monsters: Prison Slang and Nonhuman Animal Terminology." *Society & Animals.* https://doi.org/10.1163/15685306-12341516.

3. Fairclough, N. (2003). "Analysing Discourse: Textual Analysis for Social Research." https://doi.org/10.4324/9780203697078.

4. Stibbe, A. (2001). "Language, Power and the Social Construction of Animals." *Society & Animals* 9 (2): 145–61. https://doi.org/10.1163/156853001753639251.

5. Hill, J. B. & Banks, J. (2018). "Bitches, Fishes, and Monsters: Prison Slang and Nonhuman Animal Terminology." *Society & Animals.* https://doi.org/10.1163/15685306-12341516.

6. Bernard, T. J., Snipes, J. B., & Gerould, A. L. (2015). *Vold's Theoretical Criminology.* (7th ed.). New York: Oxford University Press.

7. Lakoff, G. (1987). *Women, Fire, and Dangerous Things: What Categories Reveal about the Mind.* Chicago: University of Chicago Press.

8. Lakoff, G. (1987). *Women, Fire, and Dangerous Things: What Categories Reveal about the Mind*. Chicago: University of Chicago Press.

9. Osborn, M. (1967). "Archetypal Metaphor in Rhetoric: The Light-Dark Family." *The Quarterly Journal of Speech* 53 (2): 115–26.

10. Osborn, M. (1977). "The Evolution of the Archetypal Sea in Rhetoric and Poetic." *The Quarterly Journal of Speech* 63 (4): 347–63.

11. Osborn, M. (1967). "Archetypal Metaphor in Rhetoric: The Light-Dark Family." *The Quarterly Journal of Speech* 53 (2): 115–26.

12. Roberts, C., Wagler, G., & Carr, M. M. (2017). "Environmental Tobacco Smoke: Public Perception of Risks of Exposing Children to Second- and Third-Hand Tobacco Smoke." *Journal of Pediatric Health Care* 31 (1): E7–E13.

13. McCarthy, M. (2007). "Prescription Drug Abuse up Sharply in the USA." *The Lancet* 369 (9572): 1505–6.

14. Fox, S., Armentano, P., & Tvert, M. (2013). *Marijuana Is Safer: So Why Are We Driving People to Drink?* White Rive Junction, VT: Chelsea Green Publishing.

CHAPTER ELEVEN

1. Green, E. L. W. & Steinmetz, K. F. (2016). "Up in Smoke: Marijuana, Abstract Empiricism, and the Criminological Evaluation." In N. E. Marion & J. B. Hill. (Eds.). *Legalizing Marijuana: A Shift in Policies across America*. Durham, NC: Carolina Academic Press, 19–41.

2. Mascagni, B. H. (2013). *California's Movement to Legalize Marijuana: Discursive Opportunity Structures in Prop 19* (Doctoral dissertation). Retrieved from ProQuest (3602154).

3. Wakeman, S. (2014). "'No One Wins. One Side Just Loses More Slowly': The Wire and Drug Policy." *Theoretical Criminology* 18 (2): 224–40.

4. Taylor, S. (2008). "Outside the Outsiders: Media Representations of Drug Use." *Probation Journal* 55 (4): 369–87.

5. Mascagni, B. H. (2013). *California's Movement to Legalize Marijuana: Discursive Opportunity Structures in Prop 19* (Doctoral dissertation). Retrieved from ProQuest (3602154).

6. Alexander, M. (2010). *The New Jim Crow: Mass Incarceration in the Age of Colorblindness*. New York: The New Press.

7. Mascagni, B. H. (2013). *California's Movement to Legalize Marijuana: Discursive Opportunity Structures in Prop 19* (Doctoral dissertation). Retrieved from ProQuest (3602154).

8. Initiative Measure No. 502, Bill Request No. I-2465.1/11 (2011).

9. Oliver, W. M. (2016). "Federalism and U.S. Marijuana Laws: A Constitutional Crisis." In N. E. Marion & J. B. Hill. (Eds.). *Legalizing Marijuana: A Shift in Policies across America.* Durham, NC: Carolina Academic Press, 3–17.

10. Mascagni, B. H. (2013). *California's Movement to Legalize Marijuana: Discursive Opportunity Structures in Prop 19* (Doctoral dissertation). Retrieved from ProQuest (3602154); Galston, W. A. & Dionne Jr., E. J. (2013). "The New Politics of Marijuana Legalization: Why Opinion Is Changing." *Governance Studies at Brookings.* Retrieved from www.brookings.edu/wp-content/uploads/2016/06/Dionne-Galston_NewPoliticsofMJLeg_Final.pdf.

11. Galston, W. A. & Dionne Jr., E. J. (2013). "The New Politics of Marijuana Legalization: Why Opinion Is Changing." *Governance Studies at Brookings.* Retrieved from www.brookings.edu/wp-content/uploads/2016/06/Dionne-Galston_NewPoliticsofMJLeg_Final.pdf.

12. Galston, W. A. & Dionne Jr., E. J. (2013). "The New Politics of Marijuana Legalization: Why Opinion Is Changing." *Governance Studies at Brookings.* Retrieved from www.brookings.edu/wp-content/uploads/2016/06/Dionne-Galston_NewPoliticsofMJLeg_Final.pdf.

Index